PRAISE FOR *THE 7-DAY PARENT COACH*

'Being a good parent is probably the most responsible and rewarding role you could ever have. It is also unquestionably the hardest ... and all of us need practical tips and guidance for success, satisfaction and survival. *The 7-Day Parent Coach* supplies all these needs and more in a comprehensive and reassuring way. It was a great conception from the start, and now a star is born.' *GMTV*'s Dr Hilary Jones

'I love the way this book empowers parents to tackle the daily stresses and strains that can make parenting feel like an endurance test at times. We all want to enjoy our children – not just endure them – and finding real solutions to real problems and building our confidence as parents are the best ways to help make this happen.' Mara Lee, Editor, *Practical Parenting*

'Lorraine Thomas has trained many of our coaches in the skills she teaches in this book. All have left her company inspired, uplifted and confident. She will have the same effect on you. Lorraine has a magic touch when it comes to coaching parents and reading this book will be time well spent – for you and your children.' Jonathan Jay, Managing Director, The Coaching Academy UK Ltd

'Lorraine Thomas is not only inspirational, even more importantly she is extremely practical. She will open your eyes and help you take control in your parenting role. *The 7-Day Parent Coach* is a real investment.' Steve Chalke MBE, Broadcaster, Writer and Founder of Parentalk

'I love this book, it is full of insight and fun to read – what a rare combination. Lorraine provides practical suggestions that can really make a difference. What I find so helpful is that Lorraine hones in on everyday problems that can be overwhelming – and invites parents to take charge and assist themselves in finding simple solutions to make life easier. *The 7-Day Parent Coach* is empowering – a must for every family's library.' Elaine Lipworth, Broadcaster and Writer

PRAISE FOR LORRAINE THOMAS

'Having a Parent Coach was like having a wise, older sister ... It was practical and focused and very constructive. It was about taking action to change things.' Miranda Slater, *Daily Mail*

'Two weeks later, and I can honestly say things have changed. Lorraine's talent lies in getting parents to identify, prioritise and act on the part of home life that's currently driving you nuts.' Dave Smith, *Junior*

'I feel good about my decision not to let Juliette watch 18 certificate films. Instead of feeling like a fuddy-duddy, I feel like a caring, responsible dad.' Clint Witchalls, *The Independent*

'It's not a male thing you discuss down the pub. It was good to have a room full of people talking about issues that we all face.' Luigi Strinati, *Sunday Times*

'I have lots of ideas to take forward into professional practice. Very motivating and very well presented.' Sheila Lockwood, Educational Psychologist

'The coaching was amazing and inspiring and made me believe I could do it. Life here I come!' Kate Scudellaro, *Practical Parenting*

'Lorraine helped me to clarify what I wanted from a nanny. Most of all, she helped me get the confidence to make big changes in my life.' Elaine Lipworth, *Sunday Times*

'I had a wonderful day. The Parent Wheel is a marvellous tool for Parent Coaching.' Sudha Solaiman, Parent's Advice Centre, Tower Hamlets

'I left with a clear idea of how to dispel the niggle I had, which was causing me more aggravation than I would admit to. Moreover, it was ultimately me who identified it and who's sorting it out.' Dave Smith, *FQ* magazine

the 7-day parent coach

halve the stress, double your energy
and become a great parent

lorraine thomas

Vermilion
LONDON

1 3 5 7 9 10 8 6 4 2

First published in the United Kingdom in 2005 by Vermilion, an imprint of Ebury Publishing
Random House UK Ltd.
Random House
20 Vauxhall Bridge Road
London SW1V 2SA

Random House Australia (Pty) Limited
20 Alfred Street, Milsons Point, Sydney,
New South Wales 2061, Australia

Random House New Zealand Limited
18 Poland Road, Glenfield,
Auckland 10, New Zealand

Random House (Pty) Limited
Endulini, 5A Jubilee Road, Parktown 2193, South Africa

Random House UK Limited Reg. No. 954009
www.randomhouse.co.uk
Papers used by Vermilion are natural, recyclable products made from wood grown in sustainable forests.

A CIP catalogue record is available for this book from the British Library.

ISBN: 0091902509

Designed and typeset by seagulls

Printed and bound in Great Britain by
Mackays of Chatham plc, Chatham, Kent

Real names have been changed to protect the identity of those involved in the case studies.

contents

acknowledgements

I want to thank the special people who have made my book possible.

Liz for her vision and wisdom.

Steve for his inspiration.

Tim and Maggie for welcoming me into their wonderful team.

My very dear friends, Elaine, Gill, Sarah and Tree, for always being there for me.

Ben, Roy, Keith and Ken for their support in many different ways.

Mum and Dad for always believing in me.

Joshua and Holly for making me the happiest mum in the world and for filling my world with love.

Jerry for making my wildest dreams come true and for making my life such an exciting adventure. I couldn't have done this without his love and support every step of the way.

My editor, Julia, at Vermilion for her support and expertise.

And of course all of the parents I've had the privilege to coach.

foreword

BY TIM MUNGEAM,
CHIEF EXECUTIVE OF PARENTALK

It was only when I became a dad myself that I truly began to understand what Ed Asner meant when he said that 'parenthood is part joy, part guerrilla warfare'. For me, being a parent continues to be, at one and the same time, the most rewarding, infuriating, exciting, depressing, fun-packed, horror-filled, energising and exhausting experience I have ever had. I suspect I'm not alone in saying that though I love being a dad, I had no idea what I was letting myself in for when we decided to have children.

At Parentalk, we regularly come across claims that this, or that, technique or system is 'the new solution' for every mum or dad. With a little delving, however, the big ideas often turn out to be exactly that – big on ideas, but lacking in the practical application to the daily dilemmas faced by every mum or dad. So when Lorraine Thomas first introduced me to the concept of Parent Coaching, my response was probably best described as 'healthy scepticism'.

But then I saw parent coaching in practice and had no option but to move it out from the file marked 'warm and fluffy'. I saw the practical difference it can make in the lives of parents. I saw the response from parents as they rediscovered their confidence and began to believe in themselves again. I came to realise that parent coaching really *is* different and really *does* work.

It is not just the latest fad. You can be safe in the knowledge that you'll be free, here, from brightly coloured beanbags and overdosing on fruit infusions. Parent coaching is intensely practical – real life, real issues and real family situations.

And, although it doesn't always feel like it, parenthood really isn't rocket science. The truth is that with a bit of encouragement and a little space to think things over, we can actually solve many of our day-to-day parenting challenges. This is what *The 7-Day Parent Coach* can do for you.

Since its launch as a charity, and through all our resources and services, Parentalk's aim has always been clear: to inspire and equip mums and dads to make the most of parenthood. For this reason, not only am I delighted to add our backing to this book, but also to be working in partnership with the Parent Coaching Academy in delivering parent coaching training for parenting professionals and seminars for parents in the workplace.

As someone who works with parents it's fantastic that parent coaching offers so many fresh and positive ideas. As Dad to Jack, Finn and William, though, it's even better to know that amidst the hurly burly of life as a parent, *The 7-Day Parent Coach* can help me take control of becoming the father that I want to be.

Tim Mungeam

Chief Executive, Parentalk

London 2005

www.parentalk.co.uk

Parentalk is a registered charity which is dedicated to inspiring and equipping parents. It produces a range of resources and services to help mums and dads make the most of every stage of their child's growing up.

introduction:
passionate about parent coaching

I became Chief Executive of The Parent Coaching Academy because I'm passionate about being a mum – and I'm passionate about supporting other parents in the most rewarding, challenging and important job we'll ever do in our lives. Being a mum has changed me forever. Joshua, six, Holly, three, and my stepson, Ben, 18, have really taught me what love is all about.

I made the life-changing decision to give up my job as a successful TV executive and train as a parent coach because I wanted to be the best mum possible and have a job that makes a difference to the lives of other parents. It's the best decision I've ever made. Every day we spend with our children is valuable. They grow up so quickly that I want to help you make the most of the time you have with them. I'm really looking forward to being with you on your journey.

If you care about your body and want to get into the best shape possible, you might choose to work with a fitness coach. If you care about your family and want to develop creative answers to parenting problems, then parent coaching is for you. Parent coaching is a new and innovative approach to solving the problems that affect all mums and dads. It puts you back in control, providing a positive framework to allow you to focus on solutions and to develop tailor-made strategies to achieve them.

The 7-Day Parent Coach is for you if you're passionate about being the best parent possible, committed to making great family decisions and looking for creative solutions to family problems. If you know you're doing the most rewarding, challenging and important job you'll ever do in your life – and you'd like some support to do it – this book is for you.

Taking the decision to read *The 7-Day Parent Coach* is a sign that you care and want the best for your family. It's a sign of family health – and a much more important investment than having an executive, fitness or career coach.

Being a parent is a huge responsibility – and your children come with no instructions. Your family depends on you. If you're feeling tired and stressed because you have too much to do and too little time to do it, you and your family will suffer. If you're feeling energised, motivated and in control, you and your family will benefit. As a parent, you're good at putting everybody else's needs above your own. But who looks after you?

As chief executive of the Parent Coaching Academy, I have had the privilege of working successfully with hundreds of mums and dads from across the world and from many different family situations. As a result, I've developed a unique 7-Day Parent Coaching model that has been used successfully by clients in the UK and the rest of Europe, in China and the USA. I've also identified the 10 key problem areas that cause stress for parents and each has a chapter devoted to it.

WHAT MAKES THIS DIFFERENT FROM OTHER CHILD-CARE BOOKS?

The 7-Day Parent Coach is very different from other child-care books because it isn't a 'how to' book for parents – it's much more fundamental than that. It focuses on your relationship with yourself and your relationship with your children. It provides psychological and emotional skills and strategies that nurture your personal development as a parent. It focuses on the importance of relationships and helps you to take a fresh look at your approach to family life with this concept at the very root and from which your healthy family life can grow and flourish. You give yourself the opportunity to re-order your priorities, to give yourself more time and less stress. A loving relationship is the foundation of a strong, happy family life – and no 'how to' child-care books or techniques will work without this. The relationship is the bit you have to get right, but it's often the area we take for granted and devote the least time to because we're so busy dealing with the practicalities of being a mum or dad. Like all good relationships, great parent-child relationships don't just happen. The more you invest in them, the stronger they grow.

My 7-Day Parent Coaching model works. As you'll see, this book is full of real-life stories about mums and dads just like you. They have confronted the challenges, dilemmas and dramas that we all face from time to time, and my model has helped them to find balance, freedom and fun in their family lives once again. Their stories will not only inspire you, they'll show you that you too can bring about big positive changes in your life.

HOW TO USE THIS BOOK

This book is for you, so I want you to read it in the way that is most helpful for you. Begin by reading chapter one as this will help you to identify the key problems that cause you stress and drain your energy. It will help you to prioritise the issues you want to tackle. But after that, you can decide the order in which you read the other chapters so that you make the book as relevant as possible to you. You are making decisions that work for you right from the beginning. You are in control. Mums and dads may want to read the book together or do it separately, and then compare notes. Use it in the way that works for you.

As a busy parent, you may struggle to find the time to read a book. You are too busy being a mum or dad – 24/7! I know from personal experience what a challenge this can be. My unique 7-Day Parent Coaching model is practical and effective and uses new tools that you can integrate easily into daily family life. You only need to spend a few minutes each day to see the really positive effect it can have on yourself and your family. Make small changes every day and you can make a big difference in just one week.

As parents, we sometimes find that we do things to provide the easiest option in the short term that can actually make a rod for our own backs in the long term. We've all been there. We've all done it. I want to urge you to find the time and the energy to read this book. It may be a challenge at first, but you will reap benefits that will reduce your stress and boost your energy on a permanent basis. As soon as you start taking action, you'll notice an immediate difference – so give it a go. I'm not overloading you with extra work, I'm easing your burden in the long run.

In each chapter, I'll help you create a tailor-made 7-day action plan that will enable you to take control of family life, reduce your stress and boost your energy so that you can get on and enjoy being a mum or dad. Parent coaching isn't about talking, it's about taking action. It's about positive, practical problem-solving – and as a parent you are skilled at that. That's why parent coaching works.

The 7-Day Parent Coaching format is repeated in each chapter of the book, making it easy to read. That means you'll have a clear idea of what to expect as the structure is repeated in each chapter. That makes the 'reading' easy and allows you to focus on the 'doing'. It means you can concentrate on your own situation and the positive changes that you want to make. You can focus your energies on developing the practical techniques and tools that will equip you to move forwards in family life.

By reading each chapter and completing the 7-day action plans, you are making the very important decision that you want to make changes in these key areas of family life.

If you're committed to joining me on the journey through each chapter, I know that in seven days' time you will feel quite differently from the way you are feeling now. What's key here is that together we take a small step at a time so that we can move steadily forwards to where you want to be. Instead of seeing a family life full of problems, you'll see a family life full of solutions.

The 7-Day Parent Coach also provides an effective toolkit for the professionals who support parents. All the tools are tried and tested and can be used in a one-to-one or group setting in the corporate, voluntary and public sectors.

It's really important that we acknowledge our achievements as parents. We often do this naturally to support our children, but we don't do it for ourselves. As parents, you achieve a huge amount on a daily basis – so recognise this and celebrate it.

Each day I want you to make a note of your biggest achievement. It may be something you achieve when you're carrying out your daily coaching action. Or it may be something that just happens in the course of the day and you think to yourself, 'Yes! That was great!' You decide what is significant for you.

On page 291 you will find a Parent Achievement Log. Photocopy the page so you have one log per chapter that you choose to work through, or copy the format to a notebook of your own.

At the end of each week, look at your Parent Achievement Log – and rank your achievements in order from 1 to 7, with number 1 being the achievement that carries the most significance for you.

You hold the key to your own and your family's happiness and energy. So, go on, commit to meeting the challenges and transform your experience of being a parent into a daring adventure! You have to make big decisions on a daily basis – make a great one now and start reading this book *today*.

chapter one
pest control!
be your own parent coach

DAY 1: COMMIT TO CUTTING STRESS AND BOOSTING ENERGY

Every parent lives with **PESTS**. They're **P**roblems that affect parents. You know you have a PEST, because when you think about the problem, your **E**nergy levels sink to an all-time low. Your **S**tress levels hit an all-time high. Yet it is never the right **T**ime to deal with it!

Well, this week is the Time. If you don't deal with the **PESTS** in your life, you'll continue to be as stressed as you feel now. If you keep on doing what you're currently doing, nothing will change. The good news is that the majority of **PESTS** are within your control and if you commit to dealing with them, you can exterminate them. The decision is yours. The starting point is you. You need to decide that you want to move forward. Don't be put off if these problems seem too big to deal with. We're going to break them down into small steps so that you can make significant changes in family life.

How often do you wake up feeling like Mary Poppins but go to bed convinced you're Cruella De Vil? What transforms you into the world's most wicked parent, sends your stress levels soaring and your family life spinning out of control?

Nothing unusual has happened.

You've been up for hours but you know there just isn't going to be enough time in the day to do everything. You're rummaging desperately in the cupboards to find something remotely healthy to put in their lunch boxes but all you can find are crisps, biscuits and stale bread. There's never a grape in sight when you need one! Harriet's refusing to let you brush her hair. She looks like an angel from the front ... and a bag lady from the back. You can't find matching socks for Ben so he's wearing odd ones. How can you let him go out in public like that? You're wearing your 'bad parent' T-shirt. You need to get to the shops to pick up nappies and buy a birthday present for the party tomorrow as well as looking for the card you put in a safe place. But where? Every room in your house looks like a crime scene and you've got terror tot James coming for tea. There's washing on the radiators and toys on the stairs. The phone rings. Another bill arrives but you don't even open it. The children scream when you switch off the TV. Suddenly your head is exploding and your home has no volume control.

The rest of your day doesn't get much better. You go to bed feeling exhausted and stressed and thinking about everything you haven't done today that you've got to do tomorrow. Instead of counting sheep, you're going to sleep adding more and more items to your mental 'to do' list – the one you know you will never reach the end of.

Sound familiar? Too much to do and too little time to do it. Stress levels at an all-time high and energy levels at an all-time low. You feel you're losing control and you've decided you're a bad parent. You're guilty and you're taking 100 previous offences into account.

UNDERSTAND WHAT BOOSTS
YOUR STRESS AND ENERGY LEVELS

How stressed do you feel today? On a scale of 1 to 10, give yourself a stress rating. A rating of 1 indicates low levels of stress. A rating of 10 indicates high levels of stress.

1   2   3   4   5   6   7   8   9   10

The level of stress you experience is related to how negative and out of control you feel. When you feel negative and act negatively, your stress levels increase. Your stress is a clear indication that you believe you have lost control of key aspects of your life. In order to regain control and reduce your stress rating, you need to reduce your negative thoughts and actions.

Imagine how your life would be if your stress levels were consistently low.

■ What difference would it make to you?
■ How would it impact on your relationship with your family?

Negative thoughts + negative actions = stress (life out of your control)

How energetic do you feel today? On a scale of 1 to 10, give yourself an energy rating. A rating of 1 indicates low levels of energy. A rating of 10 indicates high levels of energy.

1 2 3 4 5 6 7 8 9 10

The level of energy you experience is related to how positive and in control you feel about family life. When you feel and act positively, your energy levels increase. Your energy is a clear indication that you are in control of key aspects of your life. In order to increase your energy, you need to boost your positive thoughts and actions and enjoy the freedom that comes from taking control of your life.

Positive thoughts + positive actions = energy (life within your control)

So, the very first step on your journey to reduce stress and boost energy is to be positive, begin to take control and – most importantly – believe that you can do this

As a parent, you can feel so overwhelmed by the enormity of the task that you never get around to completing anything. There are so many things to do, so much to think about that you are constantly running just to standstill.

■ How in control of your life do you feel?
■ Are you in control? Or are you just reacting to what life throws at you?

Today is the day to change that: start thinking positively and take control of your life. Today is the day that you start to reduce your stress levels and boost your energy.

The starting point for change is **you**. We are going to focus on the things **you** can change, on the things that are within your control. You can't change other people – a challenging child, a difficult friend or a demanding partner – but you can change you. Start with yourself, the way you are and the way you respond to challenging situations. Start to take control. By doing this, you can change the dynamic and alter the way others respond to you. This will have a positive effect on every relationship in your life – and you can have more fun being a parent.

Today, I want you to commit to taking control of your life and boosting your positive thoughts. The first step is to think positive thoughts and to smile. It sounds simple, so just do it and see how good it feels. Often, family life can seem so full of problems that we forget all the reasons we have to be positive. Of course they're there, sometimes we just need to look for them. There's something to treasure even in the most demanding child.

Being positive and smiling will be good for you and it will help your children feel valued and secure. How do you want them to remember their childhood? A mum or dad full of smiles and positive energy? Or a mum and dad looking stressed and ground down by family life? What memories do you want them to take with them through life? The decision is yours – so make a great one today.

Action

Today is the day that you begin to keep a record of all that you achieve as a mum or dad. As a parent, you achieve massive amounts on a daily basis. But because you're striving to be perfect, you may have a tendency to focus on everything you haven't done, rather than what you have done.

Start your 'Parent Achievement Log' (see page 291) today. Every evening, before you go to bed, I want you to write down your greatest achievement of the day – just a few words about something big or small. This might be getting out of the house on time, making your children laugh, enjoying a cuddle, sorting the toy boxes, sharing a magic moment, having fun, finding time to read a favourite book. The achievement is yours – but make sure you write it down.

We often go to bed thinking about the things we haven't done, rather than what we have achieved. All this does is boost your negative thoughts and increase your stress levels. We need to boost your positive thoughts and increase your energy levels.

Make sure that you keep your achievement log every day, because it's an important first step in creating that vital positive frame of mind that is key to your success in reducing stress and boosting energy.

It's really important that we acknowledge our achievements as parents. Each day I want you to make a note of your biggest achievement (see Parent Achievement Log, page 291). It may be something you achieve when you're carrying out your daily coaching action. Or it may be something that just happens in the course of the day and you think to yourself, 'Yes! That was great!' You decide what is significant for you.

DAY 2: PRIORITISE YOUR PROBLEMS

We're at the beginning of our journey together. By starting to read this book, you've decided that you care about your family's health and are committed to being the best parent you can possibly be.

You can decide how you spend your time. So stop wasting time worrying about the things you haven't done or won't have time to do. Set yourself a specific goal for each day and commit to achieving it.

The first step is to find the time to prioritise the biggest problems in your family life and work out which one is causing you the most stress. Once you know this you can take small steps to tackle that big problem – and solve it. By making small changes each day, you can make a big difference in just one week.

TOP 10 PROBLEMS

Look at the list below of the Top 10 Problems for Parents. Take time to focus on each problem and decide which ones are relevant to your situation. Think about how much stress the problem causes in your life – and how much it drains your energy. What makes it so challenging for you and what is the negative impact it has on you and family life?

TOP 10 PROBLEMS FOR PARENTS
Too much to do and never enough time to do it.
Stressful early mornings.
Stressful evenings.
Shouting and throwing everyday parent tantrums.
Communicating with children who don't listen.
Overwhelming feelings of anxiety.
Worrying about your lack of confidence affecting your child.
Feeling guilty about being a working parent.
Financial worries.
Too little energy to enjoy your relationships.

From the list, identify your three biggest challenges.

1.

2.

3.

- What is the problem that you would most like to tackle first?
- To which challenge will finding a solution have the biggest positive impact on you and your family?
- What is it that makes number one the big problem for you?

- What difference will it make to your life if you tackle that problem?
- What will be the biggest benefit of turning the situation round and taking control?

Each problem in the list above has a chapter devoted to it in this book. Each chapter will help you to develop practical, tailor-made solutions to your biggest family challenges. Now decide on the key area you want to tackle so that, when you get to the end of this chapter, you'll know where to go next. You're now starting to create your own action plan.

Action

Today, I want you to start taking 'energy breaks'. Find a great photo of you and your family looking happy and relaxed. Focus on that picture and 'feel' the happiness you can see there. Today, whenever you feel stressed, I want you to take an energy break. Close your eyes and take one minute to visualise every detail of those smiling faces and to get back in touch with the positive feelings that you associate with it.

DAY 3: GIVE YOURSELF AN INSTANT PARENT UPGRADE

How do you regard yourself as a parent? Do you believe that you are up to the task of tackling these key challenges in your life – and by doing so, move forwards so that you can get more enjoyment out of family life?

In order to be the best parent you can possibly be, you need to get in touch with your inner parent and love it and nurture it – just as you do your family.

GET IN TOUCH WITH YOUR INNER PARENT

Your inner parent can be positive or negative. It determines the way you live out every aspect of your life.

If you are consistently sending yourself powerful positive messages that you believe, your inner parent will be positive. If you are consistently sending yourself powerful negative messages that you believe, your inner parent will be negative.

Those with a positive inner parent believe in themselves and their ability to be the best parents possible. They laugh, they're optimistic, energetic, dynamic, creative and passionate. Their family lives are full of solutions, not problems – and they're enjoying a daring adventure.

Those with a negative inner parent do not believe in themselves and their abilities as parents. They consistently fail to be the 'perfect parent'. They spend much of their time worrying. They frown, they're pessimistic, stressed, de-motivated and lacking in energy. Their family lives are full of problems, not solutions, and the fun has gone out of being a parent.

In an ideal world, how would you like to describe your inner parent? How would you describe your inner parent today?

If there is a gap between where you want to be and where you are today, it's vital that you begin to close it today.

As parents, we're generally excellent at talking ourselves down and telling ourselves – and anyone who will listen – what we can't do, haven't done or should do better. What you say about yourself has a tremendous power. It can be positive, or negative but in most cases mums and dads are constantly reinforcing an image of themselves as parents who just don't come up to scratch.

Remember, if that's what you are doing, you are providing a negative model for your children – so by changing this, you'll also help them to be more positive about themselves and allow them to build valuable self-belief.

Today, I want you to focus on the qualities and strengths that make you the great parent that you are. If you need any proof that you have what it takes to take control of key problem areas in your life – you are about to prove it to yourself.

Please answer ALL the questions.

■ What three values are most important to you as a parent?

> 1.

> 2.

> 3.

■ What are your three most significant achievements as a parent?

> 1.

> 2.

> 3.

■ What is the greatest challenge that you have overcome as a parent?

■ What three things do you love most about being a parent?

1.

2.

3.

■ What three things do you love most about your children?

1.

2.

3.

■ How has being a parent helped you to grow as a person?

1.

2.

3.

■ What three personal qualities make you a good parent?

1.

2.

3.

■ What three skills make you a good family problem-solver?

1.

2.

3.

■ If you could tell your children about the biggest difference they have made to your life, what would you say to them?

Sometimes the mayhem of family life means that we focus on the negatives and not on the positives. The challenges become all-consuming and we lose touch with what it is that makes us feel passionate about being a parent. Your frame of mind is crucial when it comes making changes in your life. If you are positive, you can move forward. If you are negative, you will stay where you are.

Action

My challenge to you is to think and say only positive things about yourself today. Nurture yourself by 'catching yourself feeling something good'. Feed your positive inner parent. Really focus on your positive qualities and achievements as a parent and the love and passion you feel.

Don't think or say anything negative about yourself today. Parents are great at catching themselves being 'bad parents'. Don't do it! That just makes that negative inner parent more powerful.

DAY 4: RECOGNISE WHAT MAKES YOU THE BEST MANAGING DIRECTOR IN THE WORLD

You're the managing director of the most important company in the world – your family. You achieve an amazing amount on a daily basis. You're dealing with everything that family life throws at you: personnel issues, organisation, budgets, strategy, productivity and crisis management!

Take a look at the Best Managing Director Wheel overleaf. It includes some of the key strengths and qualities that you have already that will help you to take control of family life. You may take them for granted, but they are going to be essential tools in your parent coach toolkit.

Take a look at the skills listed in each segment of the wheel. As you look at each word or phrase, think carefully about a particular time over the past seven days when you have demonstrated this skill in your family life in a positive way. You may have demonstrated it only occasionally, or on a regular basis. Think positive, not negative.

Make sure you can think of at least one example for each segment of the wheel.

As you can see, one segment is marked 'other'. What one specific skill that you have demonstrated in family life would you like to add to the list? What other best managing director quality have you demonstrated this week?

Action

Think about how much you believe your job as a parent is worth. Take a look at all the skills you have demonstrated in the role you play. Remember, it is the most important job you will ever do in your life.

What do you think would be a fair annual salary for the job that you do? Write it down.

£_____

BEST MANAGING DIRECTOR

- Which of your skills do you believe is the most valuable in facing the challenges of being a parent?
- What makes it the most significant one for you?

DAY 5: FIND VALUABLE 'ME TIME'

By this stage in the week, you will be feeling more positive and in control. Today, focus on practical steps that you can take to reduce signs of physical stress and tension. These will have an impact on every area of your family life.

One of the ways that you can boost your energy levels and reduce your stress levels is to find some quality 'me time'. This will help you develop a more relaxed and positive frame of mind – and enable you to be positive in demanding family situations.

For many parents, the idea of 'me time' is a totally alien concept. That's because mums and dads spend their lives looking after their children – and not after themselves. 'I can't do that,' they say to me, 'I'd feel far too selfish and guilty!' Well, the truth is that finding 'me time' isn't selfish at all. There are very positive benefits to all the family – not just you.

As a parent, it's essential that you look after yourself. Putting yourself first isn't selfish. It's a must. If you are feeling motivated and energised it will impact positively on every relationship in your family. Remember, you are the 'family engine'. If you're not functioning as efficiently as possible, the whole family suffers. So, do it for them as well as for youself!

What would be a real treat to give yourself? In each of the segments of the Me Time Wheel overleaf, write down one thing that you would like to do in your 'me time'. Be as specific as possible. It can be anything at all: a swim, a luxurious bath (without a child in tow!), start on the book you've been meaning to read, see a friend, watch a football match.

'ME TIME'

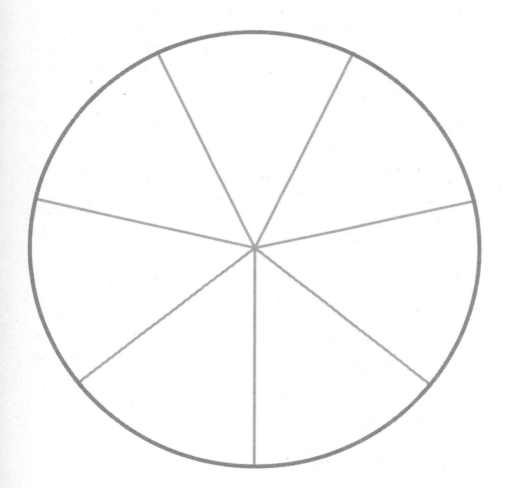

Action

Make a date with yourself this week and put it in your diary. There are always lots of good reasons why we can't manage to make things happen, but if you really value yourself, you will make it happen over the next seven days. If you need to book or organise anything, make the call today. If you need to arrange for someone to look after your children, decide who you are going to ask – partner, friends or relatives – and arrange it. Now enjoy yourself. You deserve it. While you're enjoying yourself, focus on how your life as a parent will be when you have successfully reduced your stress and boosted your energy.

DAY 6: COMMIT TO ACTION AND MOVE FORWARD

I know you can succeed in achieving all that you want as a parent. But this will only happen if you and I are both committed to each other – I mean 100 per cent committed. This is the most important journey of your life and in order to complete it you will need to be motivated, disciplined, and determined to rise to the challenge. So, before you continue, I want you to read and sign this parent coaching contract for me and then we can start on our adventurous problem-solving journey together.

PARENT COACHING CONTRACT

- I am ready, willing and able to be coached.
- I want to invest time in myself.
- I am committed to closing the gap between where I am and where I want to be.
- I am committed to implementing practical action plans that will reduce my stress levels and boost my energy levels

- I acknowledge that coaching is the appropriate discipline for the positive changes I want to make.
- I fully understand that I am responsible for my actions and the outcome of my actions.
- I want to achieve my full potential as a parent – and enjoy doing it.

Date:

Client:

Coach: *Lorraine* ☺

Decide when you are going to make time each day to read and complete the day's assignments. Put that time into your diary. If you make it the same time each day, and stick to it, it will help you to establish a routine.

If you are 100 per cent committed to making positive changes in family life, you will always keep this appointment. It is the most important date in your diary – your date with yourself.

Action

Only you can make your 7-day action plans work. The stakes are high. This exercise will increase your motivation to succeed in becoming the best parent possible – with less stress and more energy. Through positive action and by taking control, you can make great changes in your life – and in your children's lives – that will make a difference to the whole family for months and years to come.

Give your children as many cuddles as possible today. They'll be grown up before you know it. As you feel them close to you, tell them exactly what you love about them. Be as specific as possible. You have children who love you unconditionally, so treasure every moment with them today.

When you put them to bed, tell them **exactly** what it is that you love about being their mum or dad.

DAY 7:
STRESS AND ENERGY UPDATE

Well done, you've nearly completed your first week and you've made some important and great decisions.

At the beginning of the week, we focused on your stress and energy levels and recognised that negative thoughts and lack of control boost stress levels and reduce energy, while positive thoughts and being in control reduce stress levels and boost energy.

By now, you will already have started to make some important changes that are having a positive impact on you. You have now reached day seven of your action plan and by completing each of the daily exercises you will have come a long way in establishing a strategy that will help you get to where you want to be.

By now you have already:

- Committed to reducing your stress levels and boosting your energy levels through positive thinking and by taking control.
- Prioritised your problems.
- Given yourself an instant parent upgrade.
- Recognised what makes you the best 'managing director' in the world.
- Found valuable 'me time'.
- Signed your parent coaching contract, committing to action and moving forward.

You have also begun your Parent Achievement Log so that you have a written record of your most significant achievements – as defined by you.

Think about how you felt at the beginning of the week and how you feel today.

- What has been the biggest challenge for you this week?
- What is the biggest positive difference in the way you feel today compared with the feelings you experienced at the beginning of the week?

Action

Read your Parent Achievement Log for this week and recognise all that you have achieved. Take your time and enjoy the feeling of achievement. Focus on the difference you are making to yourself and to your family by thinking and acting positively and taking control. Now rank your achievements from one to seven with number one being the achievement that has had the biggest impact on you and your family this week.

1. _____

2. _____

3. _____

4. _____

5. _____

6. _____

7. _____

- ◼ What makes this your biggest achievement of the week?
- ◼ What impact has it had on you?
- ◼ What impact has it had on your relationship with your children?
- ◼ How does that feel?

Now is the time to decide which of the chapters in the book you would like to read next. You might choose to read a chapter that deals with the issue that causes you the greatest stress. Or you might like to tackle the one that you feel will be the easiest to deal with so that you can get one success under your belt at the start. This is your life – and the decision is yours.

chapter two

create more time to enjoy your family

DAY 1: TOO MUCH TO DO AND TOO LITTLE TIME TO DO IT

Sally picks up some toys and rushes upstairs carrying a pile of ironing. Rob carries on playing – totally oblivious of the time-bomb that is ticking inside his mother's head. ('Must do that today.') She changes Rob's nappy while wrapping a birthday present. She simultaneously writes a cheque for the paper bill, makes a cup of tea and asks Rob to find his shoes ('We're late.') He won't – trashing the front room is much more fun. ('Must remember to pay that bill later.') Sally unloads the washing machine and loads the dishwasher while writing a shopping list and taking a phone call. She feels tense. ('Must get to the shops later.') Sally looks for her car keys, butters some toast for Rob, makes the bed and throws the same toys back into the toy box again. ('Must tidy up later.') She gives in to Rob's pleading and puts the video on so that she can continue to feed the dishwasher. ('I feel guilty about not having enough time to play with him.') Sally takes something out of the freezer for dinner and notices Rob has taken his nappy off and is sitting 'commando' on the sofa. ('An accident waiting to happen.') She dresses him again and puts salt in the dishwasher and rubbish out for the refuse collectors. ('Down to last packet of wet wipes. Must get some more.')

Like many mums, Sally is multi-skilled: constantly thinking of several things at once and doing many more. Her mind is one long mental 'to do' list and she's constantly adding things to it at a much faster rate than she is taking things off it. She never has enough time to do everything she has to do. Her stress levels are consistently high. Her energy levels are consistently low.

Her husband, Jonathan, lives in the same house, but on a different planet. He only ever does one job at a time and even manages to find the time to enjoy some horseplay with Rob, read the paper on a daily basis and watch the sports channel on TV. He seems to be totally oblivious of all the things that need doing in the house and is comfortable in the trademark mess that every toddler brings to a home. Sally can't believe how he can walk past the ironing on the stairs without taking it up. He enjoys his breakfast without a passing thought to the dishwasher. What's more, he gets very irritated with Sally when she asks him to do things. He complains that 'she's giving me chores to do'. Sally says they both have to help if they're going to get everything done. She likes to plan ahead – Jonathan can never understand this and prefers not to commit to anything more than six hours away. 'What's the point,' he says. 'Let's just take it as it comes.' Jonathan never seems to have too much to do and too little time to do it. He's certainly never started a mental 'to do' list and will only occasionally write something down on a yellow sticky note if it's absolutely vital – like picking Rob up from the nursery. He'd forgotten that once and ever since he's decided to write that one down! Jonathan's stress levels are consistently low. His energy levels are consistently high.

Sally and Jonathan clearly have very different approaches to life.

- Who do you identify most with?
- Who would you most like to swap places with?
- What's the reason for that?

Today you are taking the first step towards creating more time to enjoy with your family. You've made a good decision in putting aside some time to read this chapter. You've decided that time – or lack of it – is an issue that you want to tackle and you intend to make a positive change in this area.

We all know just how precious our time is. Lack of time is a major cause of stress for many parents. But none of us wants to lie on our deathbed with the regret that during our life we just had too little time and too much to do. We want to look back and celebrate everything we've achieved in our time – not regret everything we've failed to do. So, now is the time to do something about it.

It's true that having a child is the most wonderful gift in the world – but no one ever conveyed to you just what a huge difference it would make to your life. I know lots of mums and dads who've said they just can't understand what they did with all their time before they had children. Once the children arrived, there was no time for anything else.

So, let's just see how tense you are feeling about time. Take a look at the table below. Read the 10 statements and see which of these have applied to you over the past week. If you answer 'yes' to any of the statements, give yourself a point. If they all apply to you, you'll have a score of 10 out of 10.

Time Tension Table	Yes	No
I feel I have too much to do and too little time to do it.		
I don't have as much time as I'd like to enjoy my children.		
Thinking about everything that needs doing makes me feel tense and tired.		
I do things myself rather than ask someone else to do them because it is quicker.		
I feel guilty about not spending enough time with my children.		
I create mental 'to do' lists or write 'to do' lists.		
I spend more time thinking about things that need doing than things I have done.		
I find it hard to say 'no' when people ask me to do things.		
I find things for my children to do so that I can get on with the housework or cooking.		
I rarely have any 'me time' when I can feel relaxed and do what I want to do, because there is always too much else to do.		
Total out of 10		

How did you score?

Score 0-4

You have a healthy attitude to time. You're doing well and should be feeling quite in control of how you are using your time and what you achieve in it. Your stress levels should be quite low and energy levels quite high. There may be a little room for improvement, but you've done well in achieving strategies that enable you to use your time positively.

Score 5-8

You score positively in a few areas, which is good, but your time appears to be slipping out of your control. There's certainly room for improvement. Your stress levels are quite high and your energy levels quite low. You are feeling under pressure and need to make some key changes if you are to take control of your time and banish that tension.

Score 8 and above

Your life is spinning out of control and your time is definitely not your own. You have very little control over your time and you are feeling negative about it. Your stress levels are extremely high and your energy levels extremely low. If you make some radical changes in this area it will make a significant difference to you.

You've taken the first step. You are focusing on how you are feeling about the issue of time – or lack of it – in your life. You are recognising the negative impact that it is having on you and on the rest of your family.

Action

From today, I want you to commit to taking control of your time. This means making great decisions about what you **want** to achieve and how you **want** to spend your time. It is not about what you **need** to achieve and how you **need** to spend your time. To help you take control, I want you to follow my 3D plan: **Decide, Discard, Delegate.** Start this plan today and commit to using it for the next 24 hours. Time spent well now will save you hours later. If you are doing something you want to do, your stress levels will reduce and your energy levels will increase.

Step 1: Decide

Decide what you are going to achieve and set yourself one goal that you really **want** to accomplish. This means you will be prioritising what is important to you. Make the time today to achieve it. Rise to the challenge of banishing 'to do' lists – just for today.

Step 2: Discard

Discard any tasks that aren't important in your great scheme of things along with any that you feel you **need to** do rather than **want to** do. Before you discard them, decide if you want to turn the **need to** into **want to**. There's a big difference between wanting to do something and needing to do it. You are actually much more likely to do something you **want** to do rather than need to do.

Step 3: Delegate

Don't do anything that other people can do just because you think it will be easier and quicker if you do it. You may be right, but only in the short term. You know that's true, don't you? If you are doing everything for the whole family it's unlikely that they'll get around to doing it for themselves. After all, what's the point? It may be difficult to begin with, but delegate ... delegate ... delegate. What stops you from delegating now? What difference will it make if you do delegate? The decision is yours.

It's really important that we acknowledge our achievements as parents. Each day I want you to make a note of your biggest achievement (see Parent Achievement Log, page 291). It may be something you achieve when you're carrying out your daily coaching action. Or it may be something that just happens in the course of the day and you think to yourself, 'Yes! That was great!' You decide what is significant for you.

DAY 2:
TAKE CONTROL OF THE CLOCK

Your next step is to believe that you can take control of what goes on in your life. At first glance, it may not seem that this is the case – but you can.

There are some things we cannot change. There are 60 minutes in an hour, 24 hours in a day, seven days in a week, 52 weeks in a year. That time frame exists.

There are many things you can change. On a daily basis, you are making decisions about how you spend your time. Nobody else does that for you. The good news is that it is you who is putting yourself under pressure and making yourself feel stressed and de-energised. That means that you can do something about it. 'Ah yes,' I can hear you say, 'but the problem is that there isn't enough time. If there was, I'd feel relaxed and be able to fit everything in quite calmly. That's just how it is.'

I want you to re-think your attitude to time dramatically. From today, it's vital that you stop thinking about time in a negative way. This attitude is increasing the pressure you feel. Remember, in order to boost energy and reduce stress you need to take control and be positive. This is what we're doing this week.

From today, I want you to focus on time as a positive commodity. Stop thinking, 'What will I do? There are only 24 hours in the day!' Start thinking, 'Great! I've got a whole 24 hours – what shall I do with it? How shall I spend that time?' So instead of thinking there's never enough time, I want you to think about the abundance of time that you have. Time is a gift, not a burden. It's the most precious gift that you can give yourself and your children.

Can you do that? Try it now. You may have spent years reinforcing the message to yourself that time is a negative, not a positive commodity so this might be a challenge to you, but it is the beginning of a journey that will change your life. Together, we're going to close the gap between where you are now and where you want to be.

Study the table below and think about how you spend a typical 24 hours. Take a look at each line of the table and work out how many hours you spend in each activity. You can decide which 24 hours you focus on. You can choose a weekday or a day at the weekend. The decision is yours.

A Life in the Day of ...	No of Hours
Sleeping.	
Housework.	
Shopping.	
Being with your children, playing, reading and so on ... time when they have your full attention.	
Cooking.	
Watching TV.	
'Me time'.	
Going out to work.	
Answering phone calls.	
Child-related tasks such as bathing, dressing, taking to nursery, feeding, putting to bed.	
Other. There may be something that is not on the list that is part of your typical day, so include it.	
Total	**24 hours**

■ Which activity **do you** spend most time on?
■ Which activity **do you** spend least time on?

Now take a look at the table again, but this time fill in the number of hours that you would like to spend on each activity. I don't want you to think about all the ifs and buts – just think about what you would ideally like to do. If you were writing your own script for your own day, how would you choose to spend your time?

A Life in the Day of ...	No of Hours
Sleeping.	
Housework.	
Shopping.	
Being with your children, playing, reading and so on ... time when they have your full attention.	
Cooking.	
Watching TV.	
'Me time'.	
Going out to work.	
Answering phone calls.	
Child-related tasks such as bathing, dressing, taking to nursery, feeding, putting to bed.	
Other. There may be something that is not on the list that is part of your typical day, so include it.	
Total	**24 hours**

Compare the figures from each table. How big is the gap between where you are now and where you want to be?

How committed are you to closing that gap?

- Which single activity do you **want to** spend more time on?
- How much more time do you want to spend on it?
- Which single activity do you **want to** spend less time on?
- How much less time do you want to spend on it?
- Which single action can you take that will help you to close the gap between where you are now and where you want to be?
- What's the first step?

One of my clients, Cheryl, confessed that becoming a mum had been such a shock to her system that she felt her whole life was in ruins because she could never fit everything in. She said she was running to keep still and letting everyone down, especially three-year-old Carrie. When Cheryl completed this exercise, she was amazed by the results. In particular, she was surprised by just how much time she spent talking on the phone, trying to do the housework and keeping Carrie occupied! The amount of time she was spending with Carrie on a one-to-one basis was actually very small. Lots of her time was spent doing the housework while Carrie was around. Very little was spent with Carrie on her own. This was the key area Cheryl wanted to focus on and make positive changes in. To do this, she wanted to cut down the time spent on phone calls. Cheryl had a big family and lots of friends so the phone was constantly ringing. Most of the calls came in the early evening. Cheryl decided to switch on the telephone answer machine and switch off her mobile between 5pm and 6pm every evening. She wanted to dedicate this time to Carrie – with no interruptions! Cheryl said it was great. She decided to use the time to play with Carrie, give her a long fun bath and get her into her pyjamas. Cheryl found she was having so much more fun that she now really looked forward to doing these tasks. The change of plan also meant that Carrie was ready for bed before the family sat down to have their evening meal. Cheryl said that everyone – especially her – was much more relaxed. The world hadn't stopped just because she didn't answer the phone. She'd taken control and was using her time in a really positive way.

Action

Take another look at your answers to these questions.

■   Which single activity do you **want to** spend more time on?

■   How much more time do you want to spend on it?

■   Which single activity do you **want to** spend less time on?

■   How much less time do you want to spend on it?

Focus on the action that you have identified as being the one you would like to spend more time on. You have worked out how much time you currently spend on it and how much you would like to spend on it.

■   How much more time would you like to find?

■   What's stopping you?

■   What can you do that will help you to achieve this?

■   What small step can you take to increase the time you spend on this activity by 15 minutes a day?

■   What do you need to do to make it happen?

■   Which single action can you take that will help you to close the gap between where you are now and where you want to be?

■   What's your first step? Do it today.

DAY 3: LOVE IS A FOUR-LETTER WORD … IT IS SPELT T-I-M-E

The next step is to start keeping a 'want to do' diary rather than a 'have to do' diary.

It's often the case that very few of the activities we do with our children ever get into a diary. Think about it. We may write in dentist appointments, car servicing and birthdays, but when was the last time you wrote down a date with your children? Lots of the parents I work with say that they occasionally plan big outings or holidays – but time spent with their children on a day-to-day basis happens in a very ad hoc way. Is your time with your children the key focus for your diary. Or does this time have to be fitted in around everything else?

Today I want you to change all that. It doesn't matter if you're a working parent or a full-time parent, I want you to start putting play dates with your children in your diary. Build on the work you have done so far this week and move forwards.

Think about what you enjoy most about spending time with your children.

- What's the very best thing about it?
- What do they say that you love?
- What expression do you most adore on their faces?
- How does it feel when they laugh and they giggle – and give you that big hug that only children can give?

Be positive. You started to read this chapter because you were feeling stressed at having too much to do and too little time to do it. Increase your energy levels now by focusing on the great things about spending time with your children doing things that you and they love to do.

If you need any motivation to help you come up with a way of creating this time then you hold the key to it. Focus on what will be wonderful about spending more time with your children. That will help to give you the energy and the commitment to create the time.

- What will be the biggest benefit to you in creating quality, one-to-one time to spend with your children?
- What will be the greatest benefit to them?
- How will it strengthen the special relationship that you have with them?

Caron came to me because she always felt she was too busy to spend time with William. When she did, she felt so tense about all the things she wasn't doing that it made her behave negatively with him. He was her second child – and a lot more challenging than his sister, Ellie. When Caron was negative, it made her feel more stressed and more guilty. When she focused on how she spent her time, Caron discovered that, without realising it, she was prioritising housework, shopping and chatting to friends over the time she spent with William.

I asked Caron to complete a Play Dates Wheel. She wrote down all the things she would like to do with William. I asked her to focus on specific activities that she could do on a one-to-one basis with William.

This is what her Play Dates Wheel looked like.

Caron decided to 'book' William into her diary every Friday morning from 10 to 11.30 when Ellie was at nursery. This was going to be their special time. Caron said she realised that William's time at home was flying past and she wanted to treasure it while she could. She decided that even if a friend called to ask them over she would say 'no' because spending time with William was more important.

Caron put her Play Dates into her diary – one a week of special time. She told me they'd had a fantastic time going for a bus ride together in week one. William loves riding on buses but they rarely do it because it's quicker to take the car. Caron said it was the first time they'd talked properly for ages and she felt she was really beginning to find out what makes him tick. She'd been more relaxed and more positive – and so had he. A result. When Caron came back to face the housework, she felt so much more energised that it didn't seem quite the struggle that it usually did.

Caron told me that the decision to create the time for her Play Dates was the best decision she'd ever made and these will always be by far the most important dates in her diary. She was so much more relaxed with William. She began to appreciate that rather than being more challenging than his sister, he just had lots of energy that he was desperate to share with the mum he loved.

Action

Now I'd like you to complete your Play Dates Wheel. I'd like you to fill in all the things that you would like to do with your children. Make sure that at least four of the seven activities that you choose take place outside the home. Involve the children in the decision-making process, if you'd like.

The majority of parents I've coached say that they find it much more relaxing to organise activities away from home because it gives them more of an opportunity to switch off from everything that needs doing and channel all of their energy into enjoying their time with their children.

Once you have completed the circle, book the activities into your diary – one a week for the next seven weeks. The date can be however long you

PLAY DATES

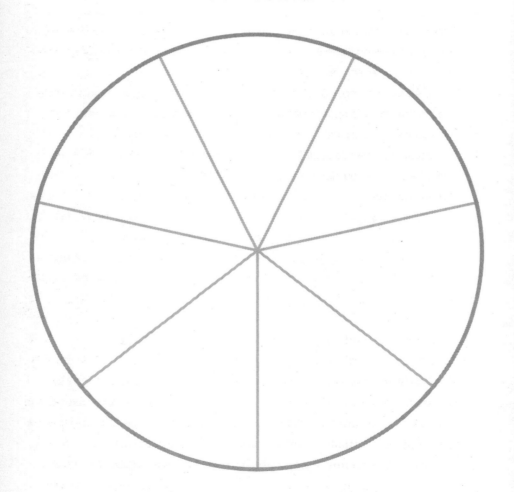

want it to be. Thirty minutes of quality play date is more valuable than hours of divided attention.

■ Which one is at the top of your list?
■ How will it feel when you achieve it?

When you book it into the diary, be specific about the day and the time. Instead of thinking I'll do it, for example, over the weekend, make a decision about exactly when you will do it – and do it.

It sends the important message to your children: 'I value you and I'm creating the time to spend with you because I love you.' This will boost their confidence and feelings of self-esteem.

Enjoy your play dates. If you really want to do it, you'll find a way to make them happen. If you don't, there will always be lots of great excuses. The decision is yours.

DAY 4: SCORE GOALS AND GIVE 'TO DO' LISTS THE RED CARD

By now, you're spending your time much more the way you want to. You should be feeling motivated and having less stress and more energy. You're ready to take on the world. You're beginning to take control of your own life again, instead of letting the clock just tick away. Good for you. You're beginning to understand that by being positive and taking control, you are actually creating more time to do the things you want to do. Instead of feeling increased pressure, you should be enjoying the freedom you're giving yourself to make decisions about your own life and your relationship with your children.

You're going to find today so liberating because we're going to give those dreaded 'to do' lists the red card and concentrate on scoring goals instead. It may sound simple but, believe me, this is going to make a significant change in your daily life.

Stop trying to be perfect. Stop trying to do everything. Stop thinking about all the things you need to do or haven't done. Focus on what you can achieve without putting yourself under stress. Focus on doing the very best that you can while still feeling calm and relaxed. This will have a significant positive impact on you and everyone you come into contact with.

Every parent I've ever coached struggles with 'to do' lists. They're either constantly adding to them in their minds or writing them down – or both. One of my clients, Sherrie, said something to me last week that echoed the sentiments of so many parents I've worked with. 'The problem is,' she said, 'I know I will never get to the bottom of my "to do" list and I feel tired just thinking about it. What's worse, sex is always at the top of my husband's "to do" list and right down at the bottom of mine. I really love him – but it's hard to relax with all the housework to do.'

One of the main problems for parents is that they put themselves way down on their list of priorities. They try to do everything for everyone else because they're fantastic carers – but consequently their 'to do' list becomes endless. You can start off thinking that having a list will make you feel better because you'll know exactly what you have to do and can get organised. But if you feel stressed because you never get to the bottom of the list this can only have a negative effect on you.

So, today, I want you to stop creating 'to do' lists, either in your head or on paper. Stop it. If a 'to do' list pops into your head, think about your children instead. Focus on their faces, if they are there with you – visualise their faces if they are not. Don't worry, you may have a slight case of 'cold turkey', but it'll be worth it. Just think of all the time you're going to save by not adding to your list. Take it a day at a time.

Here's one tip you may find helpful: challenge yourself to stop saying, 'Shh, I'm trying to think,' when your little one is trying to talk to you. When you say that it is a strong sign that your mental 'to do' list is being activated. Don't let it happen!

Instead of creating 'to do' lists, I want you to focus on achieving one goal each day. At the beginning of the day, set yourself that goal. What is the one thing that you want to achieve today?

By achieving your goals as a parent, you can make your dreams come true. Each goal achieved is a practical step towards the destination you want to reach. You are really living your family values and that is a wonderful experience.

When you are setting your goal each day, make sure that it meets the following criteria (the acronym DREAMS should help you remember):

Deadline	Set yourself a specific time by which the goal will be achieved.
Realistic	Ensure your goal is realistic and well within your control.
Exciting	Make your goal something you really want to accomplish and are extremely motivated to achieving.
Action-orientated	Ensure there are specific actions that you can do to achieve your goal.
Measurable	Know exactly how you will measure that your goal has been achieved so that you will know you have been successful.
Specific	Make your goal as specific as you possibly can.

By now you should be feeling lighter. Instead of 101 things on your list that'll never get done, you have one significant goal to focus on.

Marie, one of my clients, said that just by setting goals and thinking in terms of what she wanted to do she had changed her entire outlook. She'd even found herself 'wanting' to do some of the housework because it was relaxing.

Another client, Tom, had numerous arguments with his partner because the children's bedroom was a mess and needed decorating. He was great at DIY but he put himself under pressure. It needed to be done but he always found excuses not to do it. So he changed his mindset. Just by talking to his children and getting as excited as them about their new bedroom, he found that he wanted to decorate it. He set himself the goal – and he did it.

Imogen is like many of the mums I coach. She's constantly stressed out because she's doing everything for the whole family, including her three children. She decided that if she was to retain her sanity she needed to get the family working as a team – and that's just what she did. Her goal was a successful family meeting. She asked the family to make suggestions about what they could do to help around the house. They all really enjoyed the extra responsibility. Imogen's partner was pleased too. He'd begun to feel a little inadequate because Imogen was always doing everything herself. He took on the responsibility of putting the children to bed three nights a week. They all loved it.

Action

Commit today to giving 'to do' lists the red card and be a goal scorer. This is the way to make your parenting dreams come true. What do you want to achieve today? Make sure your goal fulfils all the following 'DREAMS' criteria:

Deadline	Set yourself a specific time by which the goal will be achieved.
Realistic	Ensure your goal is realistic and well within your control.
Exciting	Make your goal something you really want to accomplish and are extremely motivated to achieving.
Action-orientated	Ensure there are specific actions that you can do to achieve your goal.
Measurable	Know exactly how you will measure that your goal has been achieved so that you will know you have been successful.
Specific	Make your goal as specific as you possibly can.

Now make sure it happens. Before you go to bed tonight, focus on what you have accomplished.

- What has been your greatest achievement?
- What difference has that made to the way you feel?
- Don't think about what you haven't done or need to do, think only about what has been achieved today. How does that feel?

DAY 5:
TAKE CONTROL OF THE HOUSEWORK

Abbi contacted me because she was feeling stressed and beginning to take it out on her family. In our coaching session, Abbi realised that the major factor that was causing her stress was the housework. The endless grind of things to clean and the bottomless laundry pile was really putting her under pressure. It was a constant pressure and she felt exhausted just thinking about everything that she had to do.

I'm sure you will be able to identify with Abbi's feelings. Many parents feel stressed about the housework. In my experience, it doesn't matter how big or small the house is, the housework is never ending. Remember, though, that the laundry will always be there, but your children won't stay little for long.

Many people confess that housework is their biggest obstacle to enjoying being a parent.

Some parents are fortunate and can pay to have help around the house. Not everyone can afford to do that – or wants to do it. A cleaner or an au pair will be given specific tasks to complete in a certain time. The family will ask them to do certain chores, based on a decision they've made about how much of a priority it is to clean the oven, vacuum the stairs or tidy the children's rooms. Even if you don't have the luxury of a cleaner, why don't you apply the same principles to yourself?

What normally happens is that mums are constantly on the go. They'll be doing the housework alongside lots of other things – and they'll always find something that needs doing.

I asked Abbi to tell me how many hours of housework she was doing in a day. She said that she normally put in three or four hours but that she'd like to cut it to a maximum of two hours. So, she applied the same principles to her own work routine as she would if she was hiring a cleaner. She decided when she was going to do it, scheduling just two hours from 9–11am each day of the week – rather than doing a bit here and a bit there. She committed to rising to the challenge of only ever doing housework during those two hours every day – no matter how difficult it was to turn a blind eye to the mess. At the end of that time, if things were unfinished they remained unfinished.

At the beginning of her housework time, Abbi made a list of the things she was going to complete in those two hours and worked her way through the priorities. It made her much more focused on her task – and she even got little Ben to help her. Abbi also found it helped to book 'Ben Time' at the end of the housework time. She said these were the most important dates in her diary and would stop her from being tempted to carry on with unfinished housework.

Apart from the everyday housework, Abbi had some major household tasks that she kept putting on hold and never got around to doing. Just having them there was stressing her out. She wanted to clear out the children's unwanted toys and clothes and take them to the charity shop. By her own admission, the storage boxes she'd bought to keep Ben's room in order had developed a whole life of their own. She was sure they were multiplying overnight! Abbi also wanted to sort out all the household filing. She knew it needed doing but never got around to it. I asked Abbi to work out how much time she would need to get these tasks out of the way. She reckoned that just four hours would do it. Abbi arranged for a friend to look after Ben while she did this. These were jobs she'd been meaning to do for months and months. She said that when they were completed, a huge weight lifted from her shoulders.

Action

Get to grips with your household chores. Begin to control the housework instead of letting it control you. Take a look at the table you completed earlier.

- How long are you spending on housework?
- How long would you like to spend on it?
- At what time of the day do you want to schedule it in?

For the next seven days, I want you to stick to your ideal schedule.

Each day this week, set targets for what you want to achieve in the time and be realistic about this. Focus on the job in hand. When you get to the end of your time, leave the housework alone and do something else that you want to do. Give yourself a great incentive to finish on time.

You will feel the impact of these actions from day one. It's important that you stick to the seven days and aren't tempted to give in.

■ What is it like to feel positive and in control of the housework instead of having it control you?

DAY 6: LEARN TO SAY NO

One of the main reasons that you may feel your time is disappearing is because you are giving it away against your will. Lots of mums and dads say to me that they get asked to do things they would like to refuse. There are lots of reasons why they'd prefer to be doing something else, but they find it hard to say 'no'.

Saying 'no' is one of the most difficult things that we ever do. We want to be helpful, so saying 'no' doesn't sit comfortably with us. We don't want other people to think any less of us. We feel tense at the thought of having to say 'no' to someone – it's so much easier to say 'yes'. We sometimes feel uncomfortable when other people say 'no' to us, so we don't want to do it to other people. We don't like the idea of rejection ourselves and so we find it hard to reject other people.

Just think for a moment.

■ How often do you say 'yes', when really you would like to say 'no'?
■ What negative impact does saying 'yes' have?
■ What would be the biggest single benefit of saying 'no'?

Being able to say 'no', could make a huge difference to your time and how you spend it.

Simon is one of my clients. He's the father of two fantastic boys and he works for a TV company. He came to me because he was feeling guilty about being negative with the boys when he came home from work. Simon had so little time with them, yet when they were all together, he often ended up shouting at them. We took a close look at what was causing Simon so much stress. One of the major factors that he identified was constantly taking on too much at work. He was a very obliging man – and very talented. As a consequence, he had a steady stream of people filing past his desk asking for his help with all sorts of projects. Lots of these tasks were totally outside his responsibility. He liked to be asked. He loved to help other people. But it was having a very negative overall effect on him. He would say 'yes' to everyone, and then struggle to deliver what he had promised. This put Simon under a huge amount of pressure and he would go home feeling stressed. Once there, he couldn't put his work out of his mind. He knew he needed to be stronger, but when somebody asked him to do something, he just couldn't say 'no'. Once he'd opened his mouth and said it, he regretted it. His time was out of his control.

I asked Simon to focus on the biggest single benefit that would come from being able to say 'no'. He focused on the children. He knew that the effect of his being Mr Nice Guy at work, was that he was becoming Mr Nasty at home. He set himself clear criteria that he could use to decide whether it was realistic for him to help a colleague without increasing his own stress levels. Simon was amazed at just how liberating he found it to say 'no'. He said it was like a weight lifted off his shoulders. He had practised what he was going to say, so that he was turning his colleagues down in a reasonable, calm and positive way. He didn't sound defensive, he just told it as it was. Simon reported back that they responded very positively. Saying 'no' made a huge difference to the level of energy that Simon could now share with his family.

Liz and Tom were a couple with a different dilemma. They used to hold regular Parent Teacher Association meetings at their house. These had become lots of work and quite a strain for Liz, who was very sick with her second baby. The group members were supposed to rotate so that different people hosted each meeting, but no one had offered to take the job on. Liz and Tom didn't want to appear unfriendly so they continued to hold the meetings but it was putting a strain on their relationship. Liz focused on the benefits of saying that she and Tom could no longer carry on as hosts. Tom was a bit apprehensive at first but he recognised the advantages that this would bring to the whole family. They eventually bit the bullet and told the other parents their decision. Liz and Tom were amazed at how easy it was and how supportive all their friends were. The group just hadn't realised how much of a strain it had been and, of course, there were lots of offers to host the group. Saying 'no' made a huge difference to Liz and Tom.

Kelly was constantly being asked to look after a friend's children. Kelly wanted to help, but it was becoming too much of a commitment, too often. She decided to grasp the nettle and told her friend she couldn't do it any more. Kelly didn't see much of her 'friend' after that – but she said it was a good lesson in learning who her true friends were!

Action

How would you feel if you asked someone to do something and they said 'yes' when you knew that there were lots of good reasons why they would prefer to say 'no'?

This week, I want you to say, 'no' to anything that you don't want to do because you'd rather be spending your time doing something else. Think about the reasons why you want to say 'no'. What would be the biggest benefit to you and to your family? Think about how you can say 'no' without causing offence. Be calm and explain in a positive way. For example, 'I already have a (family) commitment and it is important that I keep it'; 'I will only take on what I am confident I can deliver as I don't want to let you down' or 'It would be very helpful if we can arrange another time that will suit both of us'. If the language you use with people is positive, you'll usually find that they respond to you in a positive way.

You can do it and it will make a difference. The first time is the hardest, but you'll find it liberating. You're taking control of your time and getting your life back on track.

DAY 7:
TIME UPDATE

You have now reached day seven of your action plan and by completing each of the daily exercises you will have come a long way in establishing a strategy that will help you to enjoy your time more and create more time to enjoy being a parent.

By now you have:

■ Recognised the negative effects of being a servant to time.
■ Taken positive control of your clock.
■ Created special time to spend with your children on play dates.
■ Decided to score goals instead of creating endless 'to do' lists.
■ Got to grips with the housework.
■ Learned to say 'no' when you want to.

At the beginning of the week, I asked you to complete this Time Tension Table. Take another look at the statements and focus on the positive changes you have made in the different areas.

Time Tension Table	I have made positive changes in this area
I feel I have too much to do and too little time to do it.	
I don't have as much time as I'd like to enjoy my children.	
Thinking about everything that needs doing makes me feel tense and tired.	
I do things myself rather than ask someone else to do them because it is quicker.	
I feel guilty about not spending enough time with my children.	
I create mental 'to do' lists or write 'to do' lists.	
I spend more time thinking about things that need doing than things I have done.	
I find it hard to say 'no' when people ask me to do things.	
I find things for my children to do so that I can get on with the housework or cooking.	
I rarely have any 'me time' when I can feel relaxed and do what I want to do, because there is always too much else to do.	
Total out of 10	

■ In how many of the 10 key areas have you managed to make positive changes?

■ Which of the time creation skills and techniques have you most enjoyed working on over the past week?

■ What positive impact has this had on your relationship with yourself and your children?

Think about how you felt at the beginning of the week and how you feel today.

■ What has been the biggest challenge for you this week?

■ What is the biggest positive difference in the way you feel today compared with the feelings you experienced at the beginning of the week?

Read your Parent Achievement Log for this week and recognise all that you have achieved. Take your time and enjoy the feeling of achievement. Focus on the difference you are making to yourself and to your family by thinking and acting positively and taking control.

Now rank your achievements this week from one to seven with number one being the achievement that has had the biggest impact on you and your family.

1. _____

2. _____

3. _____

4. _____

5. _____

6. _____

7. _____

■ What makes this your biggest achievement of the week?

■ What impact has it had on you?

■ What impact has it had on your relationship with your children?

■ How does that feel?

Action

By now you're an expert in creating time. Today, book in one hour of 'me time' that you can enjoy over the next week. Try something different. Make it something you haven't done for at least 12 months. It will be something you really want to do that will reduce your stress levels and boost your energy. Make arrangements for the children to be looked after – and do it.

chapter three

successful strategies

to de-stress the early morning rush hour

DAY 1: TAKE TIME TO SLOW DOWN THE EARLY MORNING RUSH HOUR

7am. The alarm clock goes off and Kate is out of bed in seconds. In her mind she's running through everything on her 'to do' list – trying to fit an hour and a half's activities into the next 45 minutes. That's when they all have to leave the house. The time's already ticking away. Call the children. Have very quick shower. ('No time to dry hair.') Not a good night. Holly awake. ('Don't have time to iron anything.') Call children again. Get dressed. Call children again. Put the toast on. Call loudly to children. Scream upstairs. Silence. Go to their room. Watching TV – only sign of life. Shout. No effect. Turn off TV. Get them dressed while they sulk. Look at watch. ('Only 15 minutes to go.') Go downstairs. Drink cold tea. Stand over children while they play with toast. ('Easier not to argue.') Need to pack lunch. ('Nothing healthy to give them.') Let them watch TV. Shout at them to turn TV down. Try to think where I put car keys in safe place away from children. Can only find one of their shoes. Look at watch. ('Time has run out. Have to leave house without cleaning teeth.') Shout at children. No breakfast. ('House a mess. Unhealthy lunch box for nursery. Bad parent! Will have to do better tomorrow.')

In most family homes, the rush hour has nothing to do with early morning traffic – it begins as soon as the alarm goes off. For many mums and dads – and children – the morning can be the most stressful time of the day. You wake up thinking all is right with the world and you're looking forward to the day, but by the time you leave the house you feel as though you've done a whole day's work already.

If you are going out to work, you arrive at your desk looking like you've been dragged through a hedge backwards. If you're a full-time mum or dad, you can feel as though that first hour has stolen all your energy for the rest of the day.

It seems hard to believe that you can feel so much stress in such a short period of time. But you can, can't you? And sometimes the weekends – when you're supposed to have all the time in the world – can be just as stressful as the rest of the week. Where does it all go wrong?

You can't change your children without making changes in the way you respond to them – and that's what we're focusing on this week.

Today, I want you to concentrate on what happens in your home in the mornings. It is really important that you take the time to focus on this because you need to identify specific things that you want to do differently. We're breaking down the big picture into smaller pieces so that we can identify what is really causing you to feel under pressure.

Take a look at the Rush Hour Stress Wheel opposite. In each of the segments you will see something that parents identify as significant stress factors in their morning routine. Some or all of these may apply to your situation. There is also a segment marked 'other' as there may be something specific to your situation that you would like to include, for example, phone calls, finding things you need before leaving the house or insufficient help from your partner.

Think about each segment in turn. What happens in your home at the moment? Your early mornings may seem a bit of a blur, but focus on specifics and this will help you. From the stress wheel, identify the three things that cause you most stress and rank them from one to three – with number one being the factor that you find most stressful.

1.

RUSH HOUR STRESS

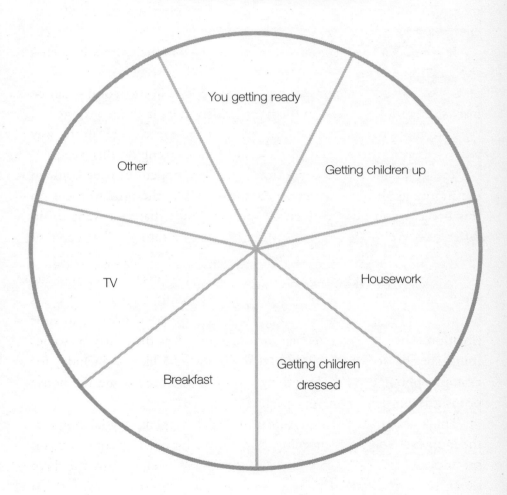

2.

3.

Action

Close your eyes and focus on the stress of mornings in your home. Concentrate on what happens now and what makes it so particularly stressful for you. What impact does this have on you and your children. Imagine that early morning scene is a video playing in black and white. Go over it in your mind. Now press the pause button and stop the picture. Let it fade and then disappear.

On a scale of 1 to 10, what does your current early morning schedule score? By awarding a mark of 1, you are indicating that there are a lot of changes you would like to make in order to close the gap between where you are at the moment and where you would like to be. A score of 10 indicates that your early morning experience is exactly as you would like it. Circle the number below that applies to you.

1   2   3   4   5   6   7   8   9   10

Now focus on what you would like to happen. Imagine what it would be like if you were giving your early mornings a score of 10. Press play again and concentrate on what you would like to happen if you were totally in control. Create the picture in your mind in vibrant colours and see the detail.

- What are you doing?
- What are the children doing?
- What are you saying?
- How does it feel to be in control?
- What difference is it making to your early morning family time?

> It's really important that we acknowledge our achievements as parents. Each day I want you to make a note of your biggest achievement (see Parent Achievement Log, page 291). It may be something you achieve when you're carrying out your daily coaching action. Or it may be something that just happens in the course of the day and you think to yourself, 'Yes! That was great!' You decide what is significant for you.

DAY 2: FOCUS ON THE SOLUTION, NOT THE PROBLEM

The problem for most mums and dads is that they focus on the problem and not the solution. They're always too busy firefighting to give themselves the time and space to think about what they would like to happen.

We're all too caught up in dealing with so many things on a day-to-day basis that we don't focus on what will make our lives easier. But today, because you are committed to making positive changes in family life, it's really important that you make the time.

The simple truth of the matter is that if you don't have a clear idea of the early morning goal you are aiming for you are extremely unlikely to achieve it. If you set off for a destination in the car without knowing where it is or the various routes to get there you'll probably never arrive.

We started the process on day one, when you focused on your biggest stress factor in the morning and imagined what it would be like if things went differently in your home.

Today, I want you to write down exactly what you would like to happen regarding your family's early morning schedule. It needs to be as specific as possible so that you know when you have achieved each part.

It may help to make a quick note of what happens in the mornings now. Then you can decide what you want to change. Here's a schedule that Mandy, one of my mums, gave to me. Her mornings were really stressing her out. She has two children, Harry and Millie.

7.15: I Get up.

7.45: Wake children up and dress them.

8.00: Everyone downstairs.

8.15: Breakfast.

8.30: Leave the house.

This is a good starting point, but to get the most out of this exercise, you need to break the big picture down even more. If you have one and a quarter hours from getting up to leaving the house, think about exactly how you would like that time to be spent. How would you like to allocate the time?

The key is to think about what you **want** to happen in the time that you have available. Yes, there are certain things that need to happen – for example, the children need to get dressed and these things need to be included. But what is really important is that you include everything you **want** to happen.

Don't feel restricted to what normally happens. Remember the point of today is to change what you want to change. So imagine you are starting with a clean slate. What would your morning schedule look like?

If, for example, it currently takes longer than you want to get the children ready because they are distracted by the TV that's on in the bedroom or the kitchen, take time to think about the TV.

■ At what point would you like the TV to go on – if at all?

■ What needs to happen before you switch it on?

■ How will this help you?

Here's Mandy's ideal schedule. By making it happen, she transformed the mornings in her house.

> **7.05:** I get up and shower. Decide to set the alarm 10 minutes earlier than usual. I love my sleep, but I would really like to have a cup of tea in peace, and the time to think before getting the children up. The problem at the moment is that, as soon as the alarm goes off, it's just madness here and I don't have a moment to myself.

7.10: Get dressed and organise everything I need to have with me when I leave the house. Put by front door.

7.15: Go downstairs and get breakfast things ready. Put washing in machine – quick clothes wash.

7.20: Get lunch boxes out of fridge (made yesterday evening). Put everything child needs to take (such as change of clothes for nursery, and lunches) by the front door.

7.25: Go upstairs and get children's clothes ready.

7.30: Decide what we're going to eat this evening. I'm doing this because usually I never think about it until just before we eat. Then I'm rushing around defrosting food and so on. It means we eat later in the evening than I'd like to. I want to plan a bit more.

7.35: Wake Harry up and ask him to dress himself. Show him where his clothes are. At the moment, I always end up dressing him because it is easier.

Have taken TV out of Harry's room – new house rule. I will explain to the children that the TV can go on downstairs but only once everyone is up, finished breakfast, cleaned teeth and been to toilet. That way it is down to them – not me. At the moment, TV on in Harry's room from moment he's awake.

Decide to set Harry's alarm 10 minutes earlier to ease the pressure – and hopefully make him a little more tired in the evening and so go to sleep more easily.

7.40: Wake up Millie. Get her dressed.

7.45: Go downstairs with Harry and Millie. No TV before breakfast – that's what happens now and there's always a row about dragging them away from the TV to eat.

7.50: All in the kitchen having breakfast. TV is still off. We are talking about what is going to happen during the day.

7.55: Still eating breakfast. I'm sitting down with the children – not eating on the hoof and walking round the kitchen. I want them to know this is our time together.

8.05: We all clean teeth. Make sure Harry and Millie go to the toilet.

8.10: I put on the TV for 10 minutes – but only if everything has been completed. I clear the kitchen stuff away.

8.15: Take washing out of machine. Write note to remind husband Ken to put washing on clothes line when he comes back from work.

8.20: TV is switched off. Harry and Millie put on own shoes and coats.

8.25: Leave house. Decide to leave the house earlier so less stressed when dropping children off at nursery and school. Five minutes will make all the difference.

After she'd written all this, Mandy said that she hadn't realised how much she could get done in the time. Mandy also made some key decisions as she was writing.

1. Take control of the TV, as this is making her life difficult.
2. Ask partner to help her with household jobs.
3. Ensure children start taking responsibility for getting themselves ready so that she isn't doing everything herself.

Action

You have now had time to think about what you want to happen in the mornings. Now I want you to write down your ideal schedule in five-minute segments, just as in the example above. Make sure you include absolutely everything that you want to be included. This is your opportunity take control and get your day off to a great, positive start.

Put the schedule somewhere that you can see it very clearly – perhaps on a pin board or attached to the fridge door. Every time you look at it, imagine just how much better your mornings will be once you have introduced this new regime.

DAY 3:
ELIMINATE POTENTIAL PROBLEMS

You may be thinking to yourself, 'That's all very well, but there's no way it's going to happen. There are too many things that will get in the way.'

Remember – if you think you can, you can. If you think you can't, you can't. I'm not here to twist your arm. I'm here to make your life easier and help you close the gap between where you are today and where you want to be. This is within your control. There may be obstacles to overcome, but if the result is worth working for it's important that you don't give up.

Many people choose to live their life in a world of problems and not solutions. As they will all tell you, that's not a great place to be. How do you want to live your life: surrounded by problems or solutions? Remember, you are your children's role model. If they hear you constantly moaning that there is nothing you can do about the problems in life – how do you think they will respond? What influence will you have on the way they live their lives?

Today, I want you to highlight any particular challenges or obstacles that you see in your plan. I want you to deal with them now and come up with solutions that will mean you can introduce your ideal schedule.

Think carefully about the challenges that need to be overcome in order to make your schedule work.

One of my clients, Charlotte, was close to tears when she talked to me about the problems in her house in the mornings. She has twin boys,

Zachary and Charlie. She had a very clear idea about what she wanted to happen and was passionate about making it happen. But the big problem for her was a friend in the street who had asked Charlotte to take her son, James, to the nursery with Charlotte's own children. They'd both decided it would be helpful to take turns to do the nursery run. But the friend was now taking advantage and Charlotte was having to take James three or four days a week. There always seemed to be a good reason why her friend couldn't do it herself. Charlotte said that mornings in her house were challenging enough, but with James present they were impossible. He was a handful and as soon as he was in the house, her boys seemed to go wild. To make it worse, her friend was dropping James off a little earlier each day. Sometimes he'd arrive in the middle of breakfast and from that point on the boys wouldn't eat a thing. This was causing Charlotte stress and was the key reason why her ideal plan wouldn't work.

Think about the three challenges that you will need to overcome in order to achieve the outcome that you seek.

Now rank the challenges from one to three with number one being the greatest challenge.

```
┌────────────────────────────────────────────────────────┐
│  1.                                                     │
│                                                         │
│                                                         │
└────────────────────────────────────────────────────────┘

┌────────────────────────────────────────────────────────┐
│  2.                                                     │
│                                                         │
│                                                         │
└────────────────────────────────────────────────────────┘

┌────────────────────────────────────────────────────────┐
│  3.                                                     │
│                                                         │
│                                                         │
└────────────────────────────────────────────────────────┘
```

I asked Charlotte what she wanted to do about her friend and James. Charlotte said she was still happy to help but that, ideally, she would rather pick James up on the way to the nursery rather than have him arrive at her house in the morning. The problem had made her focus on the influence this 'friend' was having on her life. When I asked her what she got out of the friendship, Charlotte said she wasn't quite sure. It seemed to be one-way. On top of that, the friend was constantly undermining her confidence as a mum by suggesting that Charlotte's way of dealing with her boys wasn't the best way. Whatever the subject, her friend always seemed to know better. Charlotte didn't feel confident enough to stand up for herself.

Charlotte decided to talk to her friend and explain that she was happy to share the nursery run – but only on a planned basis, with each of them doing two days a week. From now on Charlotte would pick James up from his home on the way to the nursery. Charlotte was going to take control of the situation and not let the situation control her.

Charlotte was very nervous about how her friend would respond but at the end of the day she'd decided that if her friend was unhappy, they could just do their own thing. Charlotte didn't want to fall out with her friend, but she knew the answer to her stressful mornings lay with this solution. And anyway, if she was honest, she'd decided the 'friendship' wouldn't be a great loss.

Charlotte's plan worked. What's more her confidence was boosted because she had stood up for what she wanted and tackled a challenging situation.

Another client, Toni, identified the biggest obstacles to her ideal early morning as the breakfast meetings that clients frequently asked her to attend. There was one major client in particular who always wanted early morning meetings. It meant that Toni often left the house before her children were awake. She really wanted to be there with them. Toni ran her own marketing company. She'd given up a well paid job to pursue her dream of starting her own business. She had her partner's full support. But Toni faced a dilemma. She was passionate about her family, yet she really needed to keep in with her client in order to survive financially. What should she do? Her heart was telling her one thing and her head another. If she continued as she was, she compromised family life. If she stopped, she compromised the family finances.

Toni focused on the values that were most important to her and she put her family above everything else. She recognised that if she was really living her family values, she'd be much happier and therefore much more likely to be successful. She decided that she was going to talk to her client about the breakfast meetings and explain that, in future, she wanted to meet during normal office hours only. Toni had a good chat with the client and explained the reasons for the change in a very positive way. She was highly motivated and felt the meeting went well. The client was very positive too. The MD of the company said that he really appreciated her commitment to her family. He liked the fact that Toni was clear about her responsibilities towards her children and was prepared to risk a lucrative contract in order to put her family first. The client was happy. He knew Toni always delivered and had greater respect for her because of the stand she had taken. In fact, he said it made him re-think his own daily schedule because he was feeling guilty about being out of the house so often that he was only seeing his children at weekends. A great result!

Action

Write down the most significant obstacle that could prevent your ideal schedule working. What is the biggest challenge to your plan?

Problem _____

That is good. Now the interesting part. I want you to come up with the solution. I believe that there will always be one. There will always be a way if you're willing to search until you find one. It may be a simple tweak to your schedule – or something bigger. Be radical. You are in control and if you really want this schedule to work, you'll find a way forward.

Solution _____

What specific action do you need to take to make this solution work? Do it today.

DAY 4:
MOTIVATE YOUR FAMILY TEAM

Now that your schedule is complete, think of all the people that you need to talk to if you want to make it happen. This is a schedule that you have created, but it will affect everyone in the family.

By now, you will be clear about your motivation. By making this new schedule work, you will transform early mornings with the family. You will reduce your stress levels and you will boost your energy levels. You will be feeling fresh and positive about facing the rest of the day.

- What about your family? You are the expert regarding your own situation and you are going to make this work. What will give your children the positive incentive to play the game according to your rules instead of their own?
- How can you make the new schedule one that they really want to buy in to in a positive way?
- Think about your children – and your partner, if you have one.

Let's just remind ourselves about what's happening in your home in the mornings. They're getting their own way. You're about to take control. It's going to be quite a shock to their systems until they get used to it.

All the mums and dads that I've coached have come to the same conclusion. They find it far more effective to reward good behaviour rather than punish unhelpful behaviour. Parents have come up with a whole range of ideas to motivate their children to join in with the new system. It may be praise. It may be a star chart. It may be stickers. It may be the reward of watching TV at the end of the morning routine – provided all tasks have been completed. You know your family best, so choose a system that will work for you – and make sure that it is easy to use.

In the Motivation Wheel overleaf are some of the most effective systems of positive motivation that the mums and dads I've coached have used. There is also a space for 'other' – you may have a particular idea that will work for your family that is not on the list. You know your children really well, so what unique motivational tool will give them the incentive

MOTIVATION

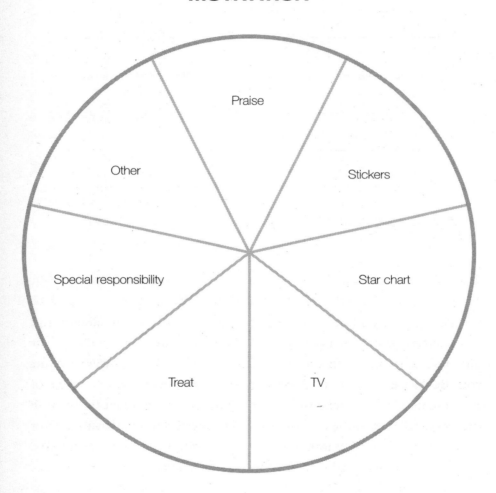

to work with you to make your schedule happen? If your unique idea is different it is likely to be better than any of the suggestions in the wheel because you are absolutely tuned in to what makes your children tick.

Take a look at the ideas and then rank them from one to seven with number one being the system that you think is most likely to motivate your team.

1. _____

2. _____

3. _____

4. _____

5. _____

6. _____

7. _____

Many of the mums and dads I work with say they started a star chart, or something similar, but then stopped using it because it all got too complicated. The system of motivation you use is supposed to make your life easier, not more difficult, so think carefully about what will work for you. Be very careful about using financial motivation, though. Some of the parents I have coached have got themselves into a real fix because they have fallen into the trap of offering financial rewards that they can't really afford. There are lots of very effective alternatives that don't cost a penny. You don't need to spend money – invest creative energy instead.

One of my clients, Jane, was struggling to get her children to co-operate in the morning. She has three children ranging in age from one to five. Then she had a great idea. Rather than tell her children what she wanted them to do, she explained what she wanted to achieve and asked them to suggest what they could do to help. Jane held a very successful family council that everyone enjoyed. This was a stroke of genius as they all came up with their own ideas. She also let them fill in their own charts each morning – a real bonus. In addition, she discovered that her five-year-old, Lizzie, was keen to be able to tell the time, and so Jane incorporated some fun time activities into her early morning schedule. In fact, Jane ended up fitting more into her schedule than she'd ever done before.

What single thing would you like your children to do in the morning of day one? This is up to you, but we are going to focus on one activity each day and introduce them gradually, rather than all at once.

When you make your list, be very specific about what exactly you want your children to do. Make sure you phrase it in a positive way. So, rather than saying to your children, 'I don't want you to leave any breakfast', say 'I want you to eat all your breakfast'. Rather than say to one child, 'I want you to help me with the others', say, 'I want you to help me put their shoes on when I ask you to'. Rather than say, 'tidy up the front room,' say, 'put all your toys into the toy box.' Remember that children are not mind readers.

Action

When you have decided exactly what you want your children to do and how you are going to reward their positive behaviour in the mornings, arrange a time to talk to them about it. This is a significant exercise in positive communication. You need to be specific and positive so that they are very clear about what they are doing.

Children have a short attention span. For example, a two-year-old has an attention span of two minutes and a child of three years an attention span of three minutes. The more focus you give them, the more effectively they will respond.

Make this as much fun as possible for them. You want them to want to do it. You are making their mornings much more of an adventure than they've ever enjoyed before. You're not taking anything away – you are adding value. Have fun pitching this to them, whatever their age.

Show them your chart or let them help you make it and put it somewhere clearly visible so that the whole family can see it.

DAY 5:
DO IT!

Today is the day. You are going to do it. Wake up feeling positive. Take a deep breath and let your early morning energy fill your body from your head to your toes. Now breathe out and focus on exhaling any feelings of stress that you have in your body. Have a good stretch and enjoy. This is where early mornings take a turn for the better. You'll never look back.

Make sure that you are totally familiar with your ideal schedule and aim to hit everything on time.

You've explained the motivation system to your children but you will need to remind them what it is that you want them to do at each stage of the schedule. Remember to give them positive instructions and tell them what you want them to do rather than what you don't want them to do. Don't be tempted to do it yourself just because it is easier and quicker that way. That may seem like a good idea in the short term but it is definitely not the way to go if you want to make positive changes in the long term.

My challenge to you this morning is to use only positive language – not only in everything you say out loud but also in everything you say to yourself. Really focus on what you are saying to yourself and your family. You only have an hour or so to get through, so see if you can do it. We're focusing on this because as mums and dads we can often lapse into negatives without even noticing it and then they start to dominate our world. Change your mind-set and set the positive tone for your whole day.

How did you do?

Action

You've done it! You've started to make positive changes in early morning family life. Think about what happened this morning. I want you to focus specifically on the positive outcomes. You are dealing with a big challenge, so take it a step at a time and you will arrive at your destination. It's a big shock to their systems – and yours – and may be breaking habits and routines that have taken years to establish.

Now answer the following questions:

- What worked well this morning?
- If you had to choose the very best moment, what would you choose?
- How did you feel?
- How did the children respond?
- What personal skills and qualities helped you to achieve this?

DAY 6:
PROPEL YOURSELF FORWARDS

Yesterday was the first day of your new schedule and you've had some time to reflect on what worked well.

Don't worry if you don't achieve 100 per cent of your goals on the first morning. As we all know, families are not an exact science. What's important is that you are moving in the right direction and that you don't give up. Enjoy your journey, a step at a time.

Now focus on what didn't quite go according to plan. What would you like to do differently tomorrow? Remember, you are the expert. Think solutions and not problems and 'think outside the square' – that is, be original.

Now's the time to raise your game. List the three things that you could do tomorrow that will make your early morning experience even better than today. It may be something you want to tweak, or something new that you introduce because you are feeling creative.

1.

2.

3.

One of my clients, Sue, found the mornings a struggle with her two boys, Rob and Dan. The mornings were a nightmare for her because the boys rowed constantly and wound each other up. Sue tried to introduce a star system but it just didn't work. In fact, it made matters worse because Rob and Dan were so competitive they ended up arguing about everything. Sue was set to scrap the whole idea.

Then she had a brainwave. Instead of introducing the system on an individual basis, she awarded stars for things they co-operated on and did together. The results were amazing.

For the very first time, they were on the same side – and they made a powerful team.

Action

Take a look at the ideas you have come up with to 'raise your early morning game' and rank them from one to three with number one being the idea you would most like to integrate into your routine straight away. Do it.

I want you to commit to implementing your ideal schedule for the next seven days. It is important that you keep to this rigorously. Every day, aim to hit your ideal schedule. Once the early morning rush hour is over, reflect on what worked well and what needs tweaking. Adapt your strategy.

I know that if you do this, you will achieve your goal. Focus again on that black and white video you imagined at the beginning of the week. If you commit to positive action over the next 7 days, I know that by this time next week you will be enjoying your mornings in vibrant colour, not dreading them in black and white.

DAY 7:
EARLY MORNING RUSH HOUR UPDATE

So how are your mornings going? Are you feeling more in control? Less stressed? More energised? By now you should be beginning to notice a significant difference in yourself – and in your family.

At the beginning of the week we focused on the key stress hotspots in your early morning. These included:

■ You getting ready.
■ Getting children up.
■ Housework.
■ Getting children dressed.
■ Breakfast.
■ TV.
■ Other.

I also asked you to score your current early morning routine on a scale of 1 to 10 with a score of 1 indicating that there are a lot of changes you would like to make and a score of 10 indicating that your early morning experience was exactly as you wanted it to be.

Take a look back and see what score you awarded your early mornings at the beginning of the week. Think about how far you have come in the course of the week. What score would you award your early mornings now? Circle the number that applies.

1　2　3　4　5　6　7　8　9　10

You have now reached day seven of your action plan and by completing each of the daily exercises you will have come a long way in establishing a strategy that will help you to take control of your family mornings and de-stress the early morning rush hour.

By now you have:

■ Taken the time to slow down your early morning rush hour and iden-tified key causes of stress.

- Focused on the solution to your early morning stress points, not the problems. You know specifically what you want to achieve.
- Eliminated any potential obstacles that stand in the way of you achieving your ideal schedule.
- Successfully motivated your family team.
- Had a go at implementing your schedule. You are using every experience positively to evaluate what is happening and make improvements. Every day is a learning experience.
- Propelled yourself forwards by raising your early morning game each day.

If you have followed the 7-day action plan, you will have noticed significant changes in your early morning experience. Think about how you felt at the beginning of the week and how you feel today.

- What has been the biggest challenge for you this week?
- What is the biggest positive difference in the way you feel today compared with the feelings you experienced at the beginning of the week?
- What positive impact has the new regime had on you and everyone in your family?

Action

Read your Parent Achievement Log for this week and recognise all that you have accomplished. Take your time and enjoy the feeling of achievement. Focus on the difference you are making to yourself and to your family by thinking and acting positively and taking control of your early mornings. The early mornings set the tone for the rest of your – and your family's – day. So you have made an important step forward that will impact on the whole family's frame of mind.

Now rank your achievements from one to seven with number one being the achievement that has had the biggest impact on you and your family this week.

1. _____

2. _____

3. _____

4. _____

5. _____

6. _____

7. _____

■ What makes this your biggest achievement of the week?

■ What impact has it had on you?

■ What impact has it had on your relationship with your children?

■ How does that feel?

chapter four
deal effectively
with the evening 'arsenic hours'

BED TIME STORIES

The Bear Family sit down together for their evening meal. This is the best time of the day, when everyone can chat happily about all the wonderful things that have happened to them. Mother Bear has had a great day at the office and is achieving the perfect work-life balance. She's been missing the children, Sasha and Poppy, and is so looking forward to spending quality time with them. Father Bear has been at home, playing with the children, tidying up and cooking the most delicious and nutritious meal. It's wonderful. Both children eat everything on their plates and even ask for seconds of broccoli. They all chat happily. Then the whole family go upstairs and Mother Bear and Father Bear give the children a warm bath full of bubbles. More laughter and fun. Then they wrap the Toddler Bears in warm fluffy towels, put them into their pyjamas and choose their very favourite story. Mother Bear reads to the children and Father listens eagerly too. Then they kiss the children, say goodnight and go downstairs. The children fall asleep straight away. Mother and Father Bear are relaxed and happy. They've had a wonderful evening with the children and now they can enjoy each other's company. And they all lived happily ever after.

Sound familiar? Or are evenings in your house more like this?

Mother Bear comes in from work. She's tired and stressed. The children are yelling and the house has been trashed. She struggles to stop them fighting. The TV is on full blast but nobody is watching it. Father Bear is screaming at the children to be quiet. The volume of noise is deafening. They all sit down to dinner. The Toddler Bears hardly eat a thing, complaining and trying every tactic to be allowed to get down. They're desperately trying to get 'under the wire' and back in front of the TV! In the end, Mother Bear gives in and lets them eat while they watch their favourite video. But even then, Sasha and Poppy argue. Father Bear is in a very bad mood. He's had a bad day. He moans about the children being out of control and tells Mother Bear she doesn't support him. Mother Bear and Father Bear argue about who will give the children their bath. Mother Bear says it should have been done before she got home. He says he's been too busy. She complains the house is a mess. Father Bear tells her she puts her job before the family. They end up shouting at each other and the Toddler Bears ask them to be quiet so they can hear the TV! The Toddler Bears don't want to go to bed and Poppy makes herself sick with crying. Mother Bear clears up the mess. The Toddler Bears are allowed to sleep in their parents' bed because Mother Bear can't face any more tantrums. Father Bear and Mother Bear hardly sleep because the children are wriggling around all night. They're all in very bad moods in the morning.

In most family homes, there is a big difference between what we want the evenings to be like – and what actually happens. I call the evenings the 'arsenic hours' and I'm sure every mum and dad will understand why. They are often the most stressful time of the day.

You may have been out to work or not seen much of the children because you've been busy, so you're really looking forward to spending time with your family. When everyone is together, you want them to have a great time and enjoy the evening.

The problem is that it is also the time of the day when everyone is feeling shattered. You may have had a challenging and busy day. The children are feeling tired. Energy levels are at an all-time low. Stress levels are high. And nobody has any patience. The calm and collected you has gone AWOL (absent without leave) and been replaced by an exasperated, intolerant monster.

On a scale of 1 to 10, how stressful would you say your evenings are? A score of 1 indicates a low stress level. A score of 10 indicates a very high stress level. Circle the number that applies.

1 2 3 4 5 6 7 8 9 10

Take a look at the questions in the table below. Think very carefully about what happens to you during the arsenic hours and how you are feeling. It may help if you can focus on an evening that has been particularly challenging. The more details of the picture you can paint in your mind, the more you will gain from this exercise.

Now complete the table answering 'yes' or 'no' to the questions

	Yes	No
Do you find evenings can be more stressful than enjoyable?		
Do you regard evenings as the most stressful time of the day?		
Do you think about evenings in terms of a challenging obstacle course, full of potential problems to be overcome?		
Do you have an evening schedule that isn't ideal – or perhaps no schedule at all?		
Do you spend a lot of the time using negative instructions such as 'Stop'?		
Do you spend most evenings 'telling' your children what to do, rather than talking to them?		
Do you find there is no time to treat yourself once the children are in bed?		
Do you often end the evening feeling angry, sad or guilty?		

Count up how many questions you answered 'yes' to and take a look at how you scored on the Arsenic Scale.

Score 1–3: You are doing well. On balance, your evenings are more enjoyable than stressful. Your evenings are certainly not as stressful as those in many other homes and you know what it can be like to have an enjoyable evening. You enjoy a significant amount of control. You may have identified a small number of specific areas that you would like to focus on.

Score 4–6: You can reduce your stress significantly by making positive changes in this area of family life. On balance, your evenings are more stressful than enjoyable and you have identified key areas that you want to focus on. There is a lot you can do to bring your family schedule back under your control. It is important that you act on this today. The more you find the thought of family evenings stressful, the more stressful they will become and the more stressed you will feel.

Score 7 and above: You are experiencing extremely high levels of stress in the evenings and there are lots of ways of improving this. The challenge is to find the energy and motivation to transform family life.

Action

You are starting to break down the big picture into smaller, more manageable chunks. You are beginning to understand what happens to you during the 'arsenic hours' and what negative patterns of behaviour you may repeat at this time of the day.

Now I want you to think about the arsenic hours from your children's point of view. This evening, I want you to see everything through their eyes.

- When you feel stressed, how do you think they feel?
- What is the most stressful aspect of the evening for them?
- What message are you sending them?
- What are they trying to tell you?
- You know how you feel in the evenings. How do you think they feel?
- What will be the biggest benefit to you and your children of making positive changes in this area?

It's really important that we acknowledge our achievements as parents. Each day I want you to make a note of your biggest achievement (see Parent Achievement Log, page 291). It may be something you achieve when you're carrying out your daily coaching action. Or it may be something that just happens in the course of the day and you think to yourself, 'Yes! That was great!' You decide what is significant for you.

DAY 2:
IDENTIFY STRESS SOLUTIONS

In the Stress Wheel overleaf are some of the key factors that parents identify as contributing to their stress levels during family evenings. Take a look at them. Now add your own three things to the list. These will be specific to you and to your situation. They will be stress factors for you.

What would you add to your list?

> 1.

> 2.

> 3.

Remember, it is the way that you respond to everything on the list that increases your stress levels. It is not the TV or the telephone calls in themselves. If you can start to take control, in small ways, you will begin to reduce your stress levels.

Now, I want to demonstrate that you have a whole pile of good ideas you can use to help yourself. In the Stress Solutions Wheel on page 81, I want you to write down seven things that you can do over the next seven days that you know will help you to feel less stressed and more positive. You're the expert in your own situation and you know the answers. The reason you don't act on them is that you are too busy. You can't afford yourself the luxury of taking time out to think about what you can do to make the positive changes required.

So, here goes. Give yourself a maximum of 10 minutes to come up with seven ideas that will help reduce your stress levels and boost your

STRESS

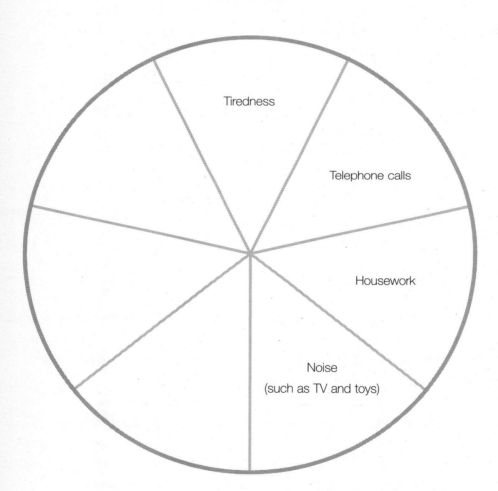

Tiredness

Telephone calls

Housework

Noise
(such as TV and toys)

STRESS SOLUTIONS

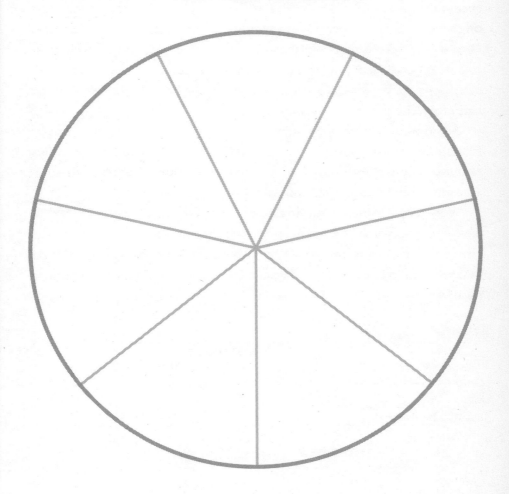

energy levels during those awful 'arsenic hours'. Make this easy for yourself. It is often the small things that can make a big difference. One of the mums that I coached had a great idea that really helped her. Nila decided to smile more often because, just by making that small facial expression, she felt better. Tom, who has three children, decided to switch on the telephone answer machine from 6.30pm to 9pm every evening. Ken and Debbie decided to have a roster that would give one of them 15 minutes peaceful downtime when they got in from work. One would take care of the children while the other re-charged their batteries – and then they swapped over. Sarah decided to sleep when her baby slept during the day – instead of doing the housework – so that she had more energy for the evening shift.

So, now is your opportunity to start to reduce your stress levels. Remember to set yourself a maximum of 10 minutes to complete this exercise. These are solutions, so focus on the positive and write them in a positive way by using only positive words.

Now take a look at your Stress Solutions Wheel. How does it feel to have come up with those ideas and to see them in black and white? Now rank your ideas from one to seven with number one being the solution that you would like to try first because you believe it will have the biggest positive impact on your stress levels.

1. _____

2. _____

3. _____

4. _____

5. _____

6. _____

7. _____

Action

You have seven great ideas to put into practice over the following week, so seize the moment and put one a day into your diary. Today, I want you to focus on the first solution on your list. Don't think about it – just make sure you do it. Tomorrow, focus on number two and so on until you have reached the end of your list. Each day it will get a little easier, and I'm sure you'll think of other effective stress solutions to add to your list.

Keep a record of what you are achieving each day with the completion of your 7-Day Parent Achievement Log.

DAY 3:
IDEAL TIMETABLE

The completion of the stress solution exercise should set the positive tone for the week. Now really is the time to stop thinking about the evenings in terms of problems and start creating the solutions. You can do this and it will make a huge difference to you.

The next stage is to concentrate on what your ideal evening would look like. In most homes, parents spend the evenings responding to what happens rather than planning what they would like to happen. It's essential to know what goal you are aiming for if you want to make a successful journey and get there, so the key is in the planning.

Think carefully in terms of schedule and structure. This will help you and your children. You and they will know what is supposed to be happening and you will all benefit. Yes, of course there may be times when you will have to adapt the schedule, but the vital thing is that you have a schedule to begin with – and it must be the one you want.

My top tip here is to start with a blank sheet of paper and create a plan that is right for you. Make sure you do it at a time when you are feeling positive and in a strong frame of mind. It's not the kind of assignment to tackle last thing at night when all you want to do is crawl into bed and sleep. Don't feel limited by what happens at the moment, and consider doing things in a different order if you want to.

Lots of mums and dads have been following the same schedule for such a long time that they find it hard to think of a different way of doing it – even though the current one is very stressful for them. Many others have no schedule at all. They spend their evenings firefighting and responding to what happens to them. Either way, there is little or no control and that's why stress affects the whole family – parents and children.

Write down your timetable in 10-minute segments. You can write the timetable for your whole evening, or focus on one key area, such as bed times. The decision is yours.

Once you have written the schedule, talk yourself through it. Paint the picture for yourself as clearly as you can. Make sure that you have included absolutely everything that you want to. Talk through the detail – not just the big picture – as this will help you to identify any challenges that the new schedule may present and think about ways to overcome them.

Imagine what your evening would be like if you could achieve everything that is on your list – exactly as you planned it.

Now give yourself a score of 1 to 10. If everything in your ideal schedule is happening at the moment, give yourself a score of 10. If your current schedule bears little relation to what you would like to happen, you may award yourself a score of 2 or 3 because there are lots of changes you'd like to make.

What score have you decided to give? Circle the number that applies.

1   2   3   4   5   6   7   8   9   10

- What will be the biggest benefit to you of implementing your ideal schedule?
- What difference will it make to you?
- What is your greatest motivation to ensure that it happens?
- What will be the greatest benefit to your children?

Action

Commit to implementing your ideal evening schedule for the next seven days. It is important that you stick to it whatever happens. Don't give up if the going gets tough. Giving up may seem easier in the short run, but you know it won't be in the long run. This is one situation where you need to persevere. Choose as a starting point a time when you are feeling in a strong, positive frame of mind. You can make this happen.

As the week unfolds, you can adapt your schedule and improve it in whatever ways you want. This is your evening and you are in the driving seat. Go into this with a positive frame of mind. If you think you can, you can.

Each evening, give your experience a rating out of 10 – just as you did in the exercise above.

■ Which evening scores your highest rating?
■ What worked particularly well?
■ How does that feel?

DAY 4: STOP SAYING 'STOP' AND START TALKING – NOT TELLING

The key to your success this week lies in your positive frame of mind. We know you've identified the evenings as one of your most stressful times of the day, so the challenge is even greater. But so are the rewards.

One of the quickest, most effective ways to create that positive framework, for you and your children, is through the language you use. By the end of the day, many parents report that everything they say to their children tends to be negative rather than positive. This is the key area I want you to focus on. Today, I want you to concentrate on **talking** to your children about what **you want them to do** – rather than on **telling** them **what not to do.**

I want you to think really carefully about what you say to your children and how you say it. What message do you want to communicate to your children? What is the best way to do that? If you were a fly on the wall in the majority of family homes in the evenings, you'd probably find that parents spend a large amount of time and energy telling their children what **not to do** and very little time and energy telling them what **to do.** By raising your awareness about this problem, you will not only strengthen the positive framework and provide an excellent role model, you will also notice a reduction in the noise level in your home.

Think about what happens to the volume of noise you produce when you feel negative and start telling your children how to behave in negative terms. Your noise volume, together with your stress levels, will normally increase. If you are talking in a positive way, your volume, together with your stress levels, will normally decrease.

We often react to what is happening, rather than what we want to happen, and this is reflected in the language we use. The children are tired, stressed and negative – and we react accordingly. If we're tired, stressed and negative, we're handing over control to them. If we take a positive lead, the children will respond accordingly. They'll be less stressed – and so will we.

When I ask mums and dads to list the phrases they use most often, many of the same ones occur again and again. Most parents' favourite seems to be 'STOP': 'Stop it', 'Stop arguing', 'Stop asking me the same thing', 'Stop doing that', 'Stop being silly', 'Stop shouting'. The word, 'Stop' is the number one culprit. You see your children doing something that you don't want them to do and so you tell them to stop.

So, today, I want you imagine what life would be like in a family world without the word 'stop'.

Think about what you say to your children in the evenings. Are there some negative instructions that pop up again and again? They may be included in the list above or they may be phrases that are specific to you. List the top three that you use.

1.

2.

3.

If the word 'stop' didn't exist and you could only issue positive instructions, what would you say instead of the three phrases that you have listed above. Try to be as specific as possible. For example, instead of saying, 'Stop making a mess,' say, 'Put all your toys back into the blue toy box and then decide which one you really want to take out to play with.'

One of my dads, Steve, found it really helpful to focus on this exercise at home (and even at work in his role as a senior manager for a blue chip company).

At home he decided to replace:

'Stop talking when I am talking' with 'I want you to listen to me very carefully when I am talking. Then we can decide what game we're going to play. If everyone listens, we'll have more time to play before bed.'

'Stop arguing' with 'Take it in turns to tell me what book you want me to read and then we can come up with a fair way of deciding which one to read first.'

'Stop getting out of bed' with 'I want you to really help me by staying in bed. If you want to grow big and strong just like Dad, you need a good night's sleep.'

These may sound like small changes but they are hugely significant. You are focusing on being positive and often breaking habits built up over many years. In the heat of the moment, when you're faced with a challenge, it's often easier to be negative than positive.

You will also notice that once you start to use positive instructions it becomes a natural next step to explain why you asked them to do it in the first place. Often when we're asking children to stop doing something it's 'because I say so'. It's helpful for you and your children to focus on the good reasons for asking them to do something in a particular way. Getting into the habit of doing this will reduce your stress levels and provide an excellent role model for your children.

The majority of children want their parents to pay them attention. That is their goal. If you pay negative attention, they score. If you pay positive attention, they score. What kind of attention do you want to give them? The decision is yours.

Action

Today, I want you to see how far you can get through the evening without issuing a negative instruction to your children. This may be a real challenge so you will need to focus. Think before you speak and pause for a second to ensure that whatever you say is framed in a positive way. There may be some words or phrases that you use a lot that you aren't even aware of using. Being aware of them is the first step towards getting rid of them.

Concentrate on reducing noise volume and stress levels by talking positively to your children, not telling them what to do in a negative way. Not only will you feel less stressed, you'll evoke a much better response and provide a great role model.

DAY 5:
PLAN YOUR EVENING BLISS REWARD

There are two phases in the transformation from evening nightmares to evening bliss. Phase one includes your children. Phase two includes that part of the evening when your children have gone to bed. You may be at the stage where you are still struggling to establish a routine (especially if you have toddlers). You may be wondering whether you will ever have any time to yourself or with your partner, or whether those luxuries have gone forever. This is very common and many parents do feel that once they have children, their evenings disappear into a black hole.

If this is the case, it is even more important that you plan your down time. This will give you the motivation to ensure that you crack phase one of the process. The majority of parents never plan what they are going to do in their down time – they're just so grateful to have any peace and quiet!

Peace and quiet is good, but it is only part of the story. If you are going to perform to the best of your ability as a mum or dad, you need to be in great shape to do it and you certainly need to look after yourself.

In the Evening Bliss Wheel overleaf, write down something that you would really enjoy doing in the evening. It will be something that you want to do after you have successfully put the children to bed. This may require that someone else be responsible for the children – a partner, friend, relative, babysitter.

Make sure that you fill in each segment of the circle. Take a maximum of 10 minutes to complete this exercise.

As you are filling in the wheel, it is important that you focus on what you would love to do in the evening. What would be a real treat? It might be something relatively simple, such as watching your favourite TV programme (only simple, of course, once the bed time routine has been sorted) or it may be something you've never tried before but would desperately like to do. These are your evening bliss ideas – not the time to catch up on everything that needs doing around the house – you cannot include housework, DIY or chores in the wheel.

This is a little like the praise, star chart or sticker system that you may have put into operation for your children. The more you can motivate your children to achieve the praise, or the star, or the sticker, the more likely they are to demonstrate the behaviour that you want them to show.

The same applies to parents. If we can find a reward that really motivates us, the more energy and determination we will find to overcome any challenges and solve problems in order to get there. It is absolutely vital that your Evening Bliss Wheel is exactly that and includes treats that will provide every incentive that you need to get to your desired goal – even when the going gets tough.

Take a look at what you have put into the wheel and rank your treats from one to seven, with number one being the treat that is the most attractive to you.

EVENING BLISS

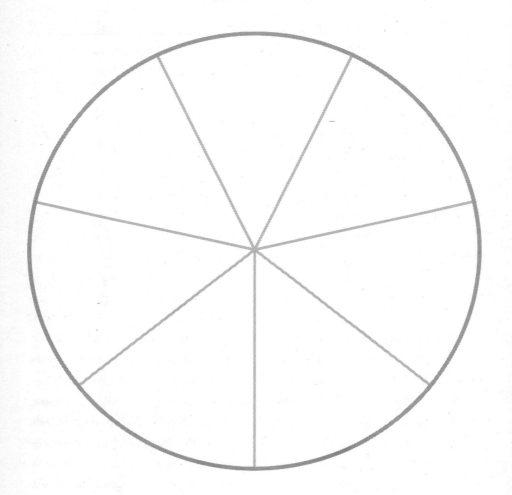

1. _____

2. _____

3. _____

4. _____

5. _____

6. _____

7. _____

■ What puts that one at the top of the list?
■ What is the big pull?
■ How will you feel when you are doing it?
■ How committed do you feel to making sure it happens?

One of my dads, William, was bringing up his toddler alone after his wife died. He was finding parenthood a real challenge. In addition, he was doing a job he didn't enjoy much. The evenings were a nightmare for him and he used to feel really guilty because he had so little patience with his daughter, Eloise. He was permanently stressed and had no energy.

As a result of his Evening Bliss Wheel he enrolled at evening classes in art. William was an IT man and had never dabbled with a paintbrush before but he had a real drive to give it a go. So he arranged a babysitter. William loved it. He got so much out of the evening. He said it gave him something to look forward to every week, and this gave him a lift on the other evenings, when he was at home with Eloise.

Not only that, William discovered that he was so good at art that he was eventually able to leave IT and use his creative talents in a new and rewarding job. That was a huge leap for him, yet it started with a small step.

Action

Today, I want you to arrange to make your number one choice happen. I want you to make sure that it happens in the next seven days, so make any arrangements that you need to today.

Whether your treat is something you want to do outside your home like William's art classes, or something that you want to do in your own home, you will need to arrange child care. Speak to your partner, friends, family, babysitter, and do whatever you need to do to make sure it happens this week.

If you are struggling with bed time routines, arrange to enjoy your treat during the day instead, when it might be more practical to get support with child care. You can always engage the help of friends, and do the same for them.

The point of this exercise is for you to really enjoy your treat. While you are doing this, I want you to think about how different your life could be if treats like this became a regular part of your evening routine. How much more energy would it give you? How much less stressed would you feel? This will motivate you to achieve all that you want to do with your children in the evening 'arsenic hours' – to put yourself back in control.

Your treat may be very simple: soak in the bath, read the paper, call a friend you've been meaning to speak to for ages. You might like to go for a swim, to take an evening class or go for a drink with your partner. What do you need to do to make sure it happens this week? Act today.

DAY 6: ALWAYS SAY GOOD NIGHT ON A POSITIVE NOTE

Many of the parents I work with find evenings so stressful that by the end of the evening they've lost patience with the children and have often ended up getting cross. This leaves them feeling guilty. They've been 'banking' their guilt as the evening has been deteriorating. In lots of cases, this can mean that at the end of the day they feel very negative about themselves as parents and about their children.

Whatever happens to you during the day and evening, it is essential that you end on a positive note. You can't afford to end the day feeling guilty. It will increase your stress levels. Parents tell me that when they're saying 'good night' to their children they're often feeling cross and frustrated. Mums and dads will replay what they've said and done – painting a much blacker picture each time they think about it. This can often be the last thing they think about before they go to sleep – and that's a tough feeling to come to terms with. Giving yourself a hard time and feeling bad, certainly doesn't provide optimum conditions for a relaxing, good night's sleep.

The more you send negative messages to yourself and to the people around you, the more negative you will feel. You want to achieve low stress levels as you fall asleep and develop effective ways to enable you to do this.

This evening, I want you to focus on making sure that the last 10 minutes you spend with your children are the most positive 10 minutes possible. This is going to be a special time and you are going to ensure that both you and your children part company for the night feeling blessed – not stressed – that you are fortunate to have each other's love.

This means that regardless of your frame of mind beforehand, you will feel positive in those last 10 minutes. If you have had an evening from hell, I want you to push it to the back of your mind. Don't give it the power to dominate your thoughts. Don't dwell on things you've said or done that you regret. You can't change the past, but you can change the present. Don't exacerbate any negative feelings by fuelling them with more negative thoughts.

So, what will you do to make sure that you have a great last 10 minutes together? Take some time now to think about this question. It is much easier and more effective to determine a plan when you are feeling calm and relaxed. I asked one of my clients, Misbah, to come up with 10 ideas for those 10 minutes – in just 10 minutes. Here's her list:

- Cuddle Ruby.
- Stroke her hair and back – she loves that and so do I.
- Smile and say 'I love you'.

- Look at Ruby and tell myself how lucky I am to have her.
- Tell Ruby what I've loved about her today. Think of particular things that she's said or done and tell her.
- Stop feeling cross with myself.
- Don't mention any negative incidents from earlier in the evening.
- Focus on what I love most about being a mum and how that is much more powerful than anything negative I feel.
- Look at her and focus on the characteristic I most love about her.
- Relax – enjoy the 10 minutes. Don't think about everything I need to do downstairs. (Often I'm tense and I don't enjoy the time.)

Action

Now it is your turn. Give yourself a maximum of 10 minutes to complete this exercise. Remember to do it when you are feeling calm and in control. This is a list you'll really enjoy writing. Focus on the last 10 minutes of the evening that you spend with your children. Brainstorm all the things you can do to make those 10 minutes as positive as possible and a special time for you and your children.

Once you have your list, put it somewhere clearly visible so that it is easy for you to see.

This evening, put it into action. You can use just one idea from your list, or if you're feeling adventurous, the whole 10. It doesn't matter whether you have had a great evening or a tough one, make sure that the last 10 minutes are the very best part of it. Even if your children aren't playing ball, I want you to carry on with your positive plan. You're playing by your rules, not theirs.

It doesn't matter how challenging the evening has been, I want you to go to sleep with your mind full of positive thoughts.

When you go to bed yourself, focus on what you love about your children and what you love about being a parent. This is a time when many parents focus on what they haven't **done** rather on what they **feel**. We're human beings – not human doings. If we can get in touch with how we want to feel – we'll turbo-boost our relationship with ourselves and our children.

DAY 7:
EVENING UPDATE

At the beginning of the week, you focused on what happened to you during the evening 'arsenic hours'.

I asked you to rate how stressful your evenings are on a scale of 1 to 10. A mark of 1 indicated a low stress level. A mark of 10 indicated a very high stress level.

■ What rating did you give yourself at the beginning of the week?
■ What rating would you give yourself today? Circle the number that applies.

1   2   3   4   5   6   7   8   9   10

■ What have you found most challenging about this week?
■ What have you found most rewarding?

You have now reached day seven of your action plan. By completing each of the daily exercises you will have come a long way in establishing a strategy that will help you to deal with the evening 'arsenic hours'.

By now you have:

■ Acknowledged your 'arsenic hours' stress levels and identified key areas to focus on in order to make positive changes.
■ Identified your own effective stress solutions and started to put them into practice.
■ Devised your ideal timetable and committed to implementing it for at least seven days.
■ Stopped saying 'stop' and started to talk to your children about what you want them to do – rather than telling them what you don't want them to do.
■ Motivated yourself to achieve your ideal schedule, with plans for evening bliss treats once you do this.
■ Committed to ending every evening positively, regardless of what has happened before.

If you have followed the 7-day action plan, you will have noticed significant changes in your evening experience. Think about how you felt at the beginning of the week and how you feel today.

- What has been the biggest challenge for you this week?
- What is the biggest positive difference in the way you feel today compared with the feelings you experienced at the beginning of the week?
- What positive impact has the new regime had on you and everyone in your family?
- How does it feel to have started to transform your 'arsenic' hours into 'happy' hours?

Action

Read your Parent Achievement Log (see page 291) for this week and recognise all that you have achieved. Take your time and enjoy the feeling of achievement. Focus on the difference you are making to yourself and to your family by thinking and acting positively and taking control of the evening 'arsenic' hours. Evenings often give parents one of their greatest challenges and you are successfully meeting that challenge – that's a huge achievement.

Now rank your achievements from one to seven with number one being the achievement that has had the biggest impact on you and your family this week.

1. _____

2. _____

3. _____

4. _____

5. _____

6. _____

7. _____

■ What makes this your biggest achievement of the week?

■ What impact has it had on you?

■ What impact has it had on your relationship with your children?

■ How does that feel?

chapter five

parent taming

effective alternatives to shouting and other everyday parent tantrums

David frowns. He knows he is going to be in for a hard time. The front room looks like a crime scene. He's seen the signs many times before. She goes bright red. She stamps her feet and David ducks as she throws Thomas The Tank Engine into the toy box so angrily that The Fat Controller loses his head. 'That's it!' she shouts, 'I've had enough. How many times do I have to tell you? We're going to be late again and it's your fault!' Yes, David knows it is going to be a very bad tantrum. He's just three years old but he's often seen his mum like this and it isn't a pretty sight!

The focus for day one is to recognise any parent tantrum tendencies that you may have and to commit to taking control of them. Take the brave step of committing to act your age – and not your child's. By doing this, you will start to replace any powerful negative feelings you have about yourself as a parent with powerful positive feelings. You can let lack of confidence, guilt, anger, sadness and regret have power over you – or not. You give them the strength that they enjoy in your life. The decision is yours. What do you want to do?

It happens to us all. One moment we're having a wonderful time and feeling on top of the world because we've cracked this parent business. We're calm. We're patient. We're fun. But suddenly, without warning, we're transformed from the fun-loving Marge Simpson or ever-smiling Mrs Walton into the Incredible Hulk in less time than it takes to say Bob The Builder!

What presses your button? What makes you shout or throw parent tantrums?

It wasn't a major incident. Your children didn't put your purse down the toilet or make an emergency 999 call while you were making coffee.

Nothing unusual has happened. It's just an ordinary day.

She isn't happy when you switch off her favourite video. But you have to get out. It takes five minutes to get her into the car. It's difficult when both your child and the car seat straps have minds of their own. To top it all, she steadfastly refuses to let go of you when you reach the nursery and is clinging on for dear life sobbing and screaming, 'Don't leave me!' You feel everyone's eyes are on you. You imagine what's going through her head: 'If you really loved me, Mum, you wouldn't leave me here.' You're going to be late. You are a melting pot of powerful emotions. You feel guilty, frustrated, angry and anxious. Your stress levels are rising.

You can't even remember why, but suddenly you snap. Your toddler throws a wobbly. She shouts and you shout back – but much louder. Before you know it, you are throwing a tantrum in a league of its own.

It's often the little things that can bring out the worst in us and small incidents escalate into major wars. Welcome to the world of parent tantrums.

Of course, this isn't what you want to happen. If you were writing the script it would be very different. But your children have different ideas, and they're playing by their rules, not yours.

TOP SIX PARENT TANTRUM SIGNS

We all know what it's like to see our children have a tantrum and over the years we've become experts at recognising the warning signs. They say that early childhood is a dress rehearsal for the teenage years. That's why it is so important to regain control while they're young. A child of any age can throw a pretty impressive tantrum and as a parent it can make us feel helpless and inadequate because we cannot control what is happening.

But the reality is that many parents throw tantrums too. Do you recognise the warning signs in yourself? It takes a great deal of courage to admit that you lose control and say and do things that you regret, especially where your children are concerned.

A parent tantrum is powerful. It can have a significant negative effect, not only on the way we feel about ourselves but also on the way we feel about our children. It can also affect the way they feel about us and about themselves. That's why it is vital to focus on this area and bring about some really positive changes.

Parent tantrums have an extremely stressful effect on you. They happen when you are losing control of yourself and the situation. In most cases, you say negative things or perform negative actions.By turning the situation around and taking control, however, you can boost your energy levels with positive words and positive actions.

Six key signs of a parent tantrum are listed below. The first step is to think carefully about what has been happening in your life over the past week. Take a look at each sign in turn and make a note of how often you've experienced it in the past week.

It's really important that you are honest with yourself here, so take your time to get this absolutely right. If you are going to make positive changes in this area of your life, you need to be realistic about the current situation. You can then compare this with how you are feeling at the end of the week, and you will know that you have made progress.

Choose one box for each parent tantrum sign from the following options:

1. Once or twice a week.
2. Once a day.
3. Twice a day.
4. Three or more times a day.

TOP SIX PARENT TANTRUM SIGNS	Once or twice a week	Once a day	Twice a day	Three or more times a day
1. You experience negative feelings about yourself as a parent, including guilt, anger, sadness, regret and lack of confidence.				
2. You shout or raise your voice, saying critical or negative things to your children that you would not say if calm.				
3. You experience negative feelings towards your children and blame them for your loss of control.				
4. You pay negative attention to your children and it usually involves 'telling off'.				
5. You lose control and start acting your children's age and not your own.				
6. You feel signs of physical stress and tension.				

■ Which one makes you feel worse than all the others?
■ What's the reason for that?

Every parent I've coached has had a parent tantrum at some time or other. If there's one thing that being a parent coach has taught me, it's that there's no such thing as a perfect child, and no such thing as a perfect parent! Don't waste time feeling bad and admit that you are only human. You can't change the past. But you can change the present and the future.

We all know just how challenging children's behaviour can be at times. You can't change your children's challenging behaviour overnight because it is outside your control. They control the way they behave, not you. They are determined to have their own way and the reality is that they won't do what you want them to do just because you tell them to. If only it were that easy.

But you *can* change the way you respond to their challenging behaviour. By making positive changes in the way you behave, you can change the dynamics of your relationship. This, in turn, will change the way they respond to you and will have a significant and positive impact on their behaviour.

It's important to remember that you are your children's most important role model. Much of their behaviour is caught, not taught and they will take their lead from you. If they see you throwing parent tantrums to get your own way, they're much more likely to throw tantrums themselves.

Remember, the key to success is in believing you can do it. You know your family best and Parent Coaching is all about developing a practical strategy that works for you. Every parent and every child is different.

If you have parent tantrums – occasionally or frequently – and you'd like to do something about it, here is a practical 7-day action plan with simple techniques that you can integrate into your everyday family life. If you follow the plan, I know that you can bring about significant changes in the coming week.

Action

Commit to acting your age – not theirs. You won't change their behaviour by shouting but you can change their behaviour by setting a great example. If you shout and stamp your feet to get your own way, that's what they will learn to do. If you're calm and positive, they'll want to be like that too.

My challenge to you is to see how far through the day you can get without throwing a parent tantrum. I want you to keep calm and not shout or raise your voice. If you only manage to get to 6.30am, don't give up. Just try to get through to 6.45am tomorrow. Take small steps and you can get to where you want to be. Over the next seven days, I want you to get through at least one whole day without shouting or throwing a tantrum. You can do this.

■ How does it feel to be in control?

■ How do your children respond?

■ What positive impact is it having on you and your family?

It's really important that we acknowledge our achievements as parents. Each day I want you to make a note of your biggest achievement (see Parent Achievement Log, page 291). It may be something you achieve when you're carrying out your daily coaching action. Or it may be something that just happens in the course of the day and you think to yourself, 'Yes! That was great!' You decide what is significant for you.

DAY 2:
BE THE PARENT YOU WANT TO BE

The next step is to decide how much you want to stop shouting and come up with a plan that will help you control yourself. The children's behaviour may be winding you up, but at the end of the day, you have control – or lack of it. They don't make you shout and say things you'll regret later. You do. It's hard but it's **your** decision. Do you want to do something about it or not? Being a parent is a steep learning curve so recognise this. There's no reason why you should have all the answers, but you can do your best.

Take a few minutes to answer the following three questions. Think carefully about the answers and write them down, if this helps.

■ What is the single biggest reason that motivates you to want to reduce the number of times you shout and have other parent tantrums?

■ How will you feel when you achieve this?

■ On a scale of 1 to 10, with 10 being very committed, how committed are you to achieving this? Circle the number that applies.

1 2 3 4 5 6 7 8 9 10

From today, it is important that you commit to believing in yourself as a parent. After all, your children do. In the first chapter, we focused on how important it is to nurture your positive inner parent. This is something you want to do if you are going to reduce stress and boost your energy. You are in control, so be the parent you want to be and live your life accordingly.

Think of a particular time when you have really shouted or had a memorable parent tantrum.

- ■ What happened that made you lose your control?
- ■ How did it feel?
- ■ Who do you become when you have a tantrum?

When I ask mums and dads this last question they come up with a long list of interesting characters. One mum said she felt just like Ron Weasley's mum in Harry Potter (do you remember Ron's face when he received that dreadful 'Howler' in the owl post?) because she would just lose control and rant for what seemed like hours. One of the dads that I was coaching assured me that he became Basil Fawlty because he used to get absolutely exasperated at the smallest thing and throw a major tantrum that competed with his two-year-old's. Unfortunately, his two-year-old won the battle of wills.

When faced with challenging behaviour in your children, what characteristics would you like to demonstrate and how would you like to handle the situation? Again, when I ask the mums and dads I work with, they find it helpful to focus on particular characters with qualities they'd like to emulate. Some of the favourites are Mrs Walton and Marge Simpson from the popular TV programmes, and Mary Poppins. Or perhaps you just want to be the 'real you'.

What skills and qualities do you want to demonstrate: love, calm, compassion, control, respect, integrity, fun, fairness? The decision is yours.

In the Ideal Parent Wheel overleaf, write down one word or phrase in each segment to record the qualities you want to demonstrate on a daily basis.

Once you have completed the wheel, rank the qualities from one to seven with number one being the quality that is most important to you.

IDEAL PARENT

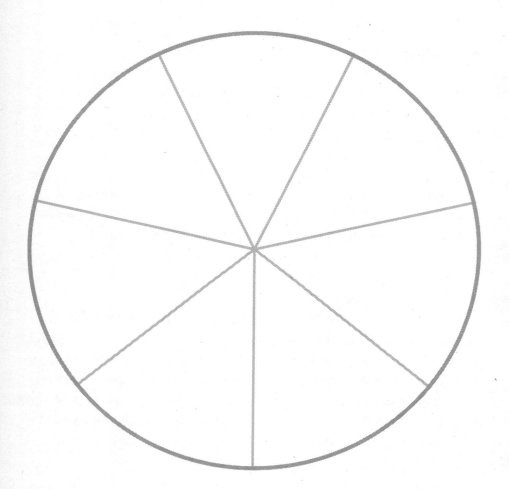

1. _____

2. _____

3. _____

4. _____

5. _____

6. _____

7. _____

Action

Commit today to raising your game and boosting those skills and qualities in everything you do with your children and not just when you're dealing with tantrums. That's the parent you want to be, so be it. If you think you can, you can. If you think you can't, it is only you that's stopping you.

Take a look at the qualities you've identified. You've listed the seven that are most important to you. Every day this week, I want you to focus on a specific one and boost it in your everyday life. I want you to really 'live' and 'feel' that quality in everything you think and say and do. By the end of the week, you will have improved your ideal parent status in seven different ways.

Remember too, to complete your Parent Achievement Log (see page 291) at the end of every day. Make a note of one specific thing that you've achieved in the day. There will be lots – you decide which is most significant for you.

DAY 3: GIVE TANTRUM WORDS THE RED CARD

The next step is to focus on specific times when you shout or raise your voice, saying critical or negative things to your children that you would not say if you were calm.

In the Tantrum Words Wheel opposite, write down the seven commonest things that you say to your children when you are having a tantrum.

Some of the commonest words and phrases that feature in coaching sessions with parents are, 'Just do it', 'Do as I tell you', 'No!', 'I won't tell you again', 'Why can't you be more like ....?', 'Because I said so', 'Grow up', 'Stop shouting', 'Don't be rude', 'That's it, you're not going to ...', 'Why do you make me so angry?' Everybody's wheel will be different. Choose the words and phrases that you use most often and then regret saying; the words and phrases that you would most like to remove from your vocabulary for ever.

Once you have completed your wheel, rank the words or phrases that you would most like to eradicate from your vocabulary, from one to seven, with number one being the word or phrase you would most like to get rid of.

1. _____

2. _____

3. _____

4. _____

5. _____

6. _____

7. _____

TANTRUM WORDS

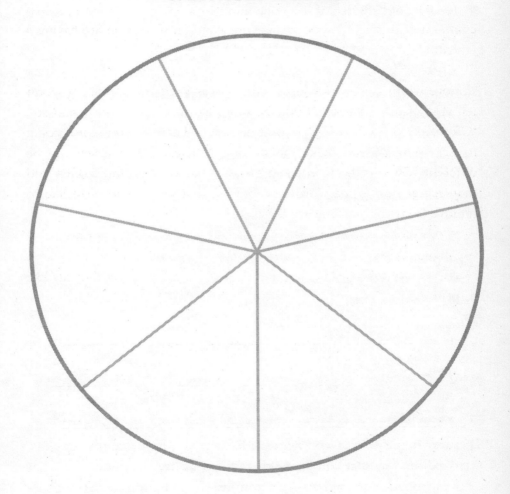

You may find it helpful to ask yourself the following questions:

- How do you feel when you say them?
- How do you think your children feel?
- What message are you sending?
- What message do you want to send?
- How would you feel if someone said them to you?

Action

From today, commit to giving tantrum words and phrases the 'red card' and removing them from your vocabulary. You have identified your top seven so act today to start eradicating them. Keep a diary of what you achieve. Once you have completed one day without saying your number one word or phrase on your Tantrum Word Wheel, move on to the second word or phrase and repeat the exercise.

- When you're not using your tantrum 'red card' words and phrases – what words and phrases are you using to replace them?
- How do your children respond?
- How does it feel?

DAY 4:
SEE THE CHILD YOU LOVE

The next step is to focus on negative feelings you have about your children and the way that you blame them for your loss of control.

Remember, your children may know just which buttons to press. They may know exactly how to wind you up. They may push you to the edge. But at the end of the day, it is you who decides how to respond to their behaviour. It is you and not they who makes you throw a parent tantrum.

One of the challenges for parents is that when they are in the throes of a tantrum they can only see the negatives in their children. It's important to recognise that it's your children's behaviour that is challenging not your children themselves. Make a clear distinction between who they are and what they are doing.

When you are having a parent tantrum, what do you see when you look at your child? How negative are your feelings about them? The mums and dads that I work with often say that although they love their children, they don't actually like them. In fact, it's the behaviour they don't like, not their children.

How committed are you to replacing those negative feelings with positive ones – even when your children's behaviour pushes you to the edge?

Don't take anything they say or do personally. This is about them learning to be independent. It's not about you. See life through their eyes and try to understand what they might be trying to communicate.

Close your eyes and focus on your children. If you have more than one, focus on one at a time. Create as clear a picture as you can of them. See them vividly in colour. See the detail in their faces. What is it you love most about the way they smile and laugh?

Sometimes, when children are behaving in a particularly challenging way, parents can struggle to get back in touch with these positive feelings for their children and often blame their children for making them lose their temper.

There will be lots of things you love about your children. Take some time and focus on what it is you really, really love about them? In each of the segments of the wheel overleaf, write down one thing that you love about your children. Try to be as specific as you can possibly be. So, if they make you laugh, what is it exactly that they do that makes you laugh?

Once you've completed the wheel, tell your children what you love about them. While you're talking, think about which one of these positive attributes brings out the most powerful, positive feelings in you.

One of the dads I was coaching, Ram, was shouting at his children regularly. He said he felt a distance between him and them. He loved his children, but was really struggling with the challenge of being a dad and getting back in touch with the strong feelings of love he had for them. I asked him to think what he could do that would help him to feel that love – even in the most difficult situations. He thought for a few minutes and

LOVE MY CHILD

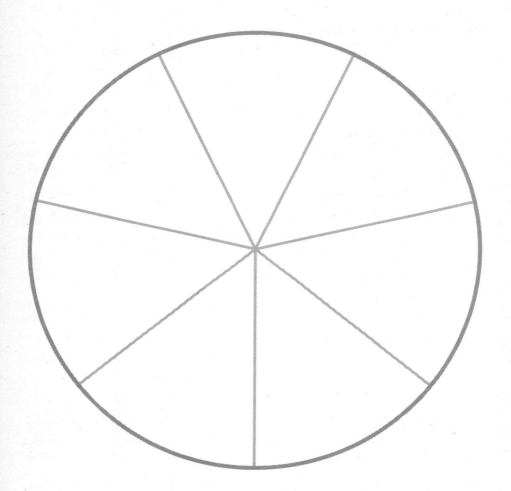

then told me. 'I know exactly what I want to do,' he said. 'Whenever I see them and I am finding their behaviour difficult, I will imagine that this is the last time I will ever see them and I know that will help me to appreciate and love them more. I will think about what I would say to them if this was my very last opportunity to tell them I love them.' He was thinking 'outside the box'. This was a radical and great decision. Ram reported back that framing the situation like this really helped him to get his priorities right. It brought about big changes in him – and in the children.

Action

When you feel you are losing control, don't see a difficult child who's deliberately refusing to obey you, see the child you love. Focus on the strongest positive feeling that you identified in your Love My Child Wheel and this will help you.

I want you to re-frame the picture you have of your children and see them differently. Instead of seeing a difficult child who is being naughty and challenging your authority, see a little person who loves you unconditionally. Don't take anything your children say or do personally. Imagine that they're not being difficult, they're trying to assert their independence, so think of ways you can help them to do this. Remember, it is their behaviour that you feel negative about, not them.

Think positive, and when you look at them, see the children you love.

DAY 5:
PLAY BY YOUR RULES – NOT THEIRS

At the moment, your children want your attention and you are giving it to them. You may be shouting or telling them off – but it's attention all the same.

Today you are going to make significant changes and turn the negative attention you are giving your children into positive attention. Play the game by your rules instead of theirs. Ignore their challenging behaviour.

Instead, catch them 'red-handed' being good. They'll soon understand that if they throw a tantrum they get no attention. If they behave well, they get great attention.

Remember, they're not in control – you are.

From now on, I'd like you to work hard at reducing the number of times you tell them off and increasing the number of times that you catch them doing something good.

- What do you do more of at the moment, telling them off or praising them?
- How often over the past 24 hours have you told them off?
- How often have you praised them?

In many ways, our children are no different from us. They want attention. Your children may feel so desperate for your attention that they're even happy if it's negative and not positive attention. They don't mind being told off because at least it means they've got your attention. How much better, then, if you can transform that negative attention into positive attention. Think about how you feel when you are criticised and how you feel when you receive praise.

As parents, we are often so busy that we focus on what our children are doing wrong, rather than praising them for doing something right. If they're behaving, we often let it pass without comment. If they're misbehaving, it dominates our world.

Action

Today, I want you to focus on giving your children only positive attention. If they aren't behaving well, ignore them. If they are behaving well, praise them – catch them 'red-handed' being good. Each time you praise them, be as specific as you can about what you are praising them for.

- How does it feel?
- How do they respond?

DAY 6:
DAILY PARENT TANTRUM HOTSPOTS

The next step is to focus on the times when your parent tantrums are at their worst and concentrate on some creative problem-solving that will help you to reduce the stress at particularly difficult times. When your tantrums are at their worst, you are very much in danger of acting your children's age and not your own. Many mums and dads start to describe what happens when they lose control – and then it suddenly dawns on them – 'I've just realized what I'm doing, I'm acting like them.' Often, this had never occurred to them before they started to recount in detail what happens when they hit a 'Tantrum Hotspot'. Parents' lack of control means they stop acting like adults and start acting like children. Instead of their children copying them – they're copying their children. Think about what it's like when your children argue with another child. That's what is happening to you. No wonder it's stressful.

Your worst parent tantrums may occur more frequently at particular times of the day, for example, bed times, meal times or in the early mornings. One of my mothers was in tears when she told me about her very worst time – the hour when she gets in from work. It was the time when she most wanted to enjoy being with the children but everyone was always tired and stressed and tempers flared. I'm sure her experience strikes a chord with you. There may be certain things that 'trigger' your tantrums, for example, stand-offs between you and your children over getting into the buggy, watching TV, sharing toys or getting dressed.

Your daily parent tantrum hotspots may occur when you are feeling particularly tired or stressed. There may be certain things that your children do or say that 'push your tantrum button'.

Identify the top three times when your parent tantrums are at their worst. This is to help you break down the big picture in your home into specific incidents.

1.

> 2.

> 3.

- What difference will it make to you and your family if you can turn these situations around?
- What will be the biggest benefit of taking control and acting positively?

Focus on your number one – your most challenging situation. Think about what happens now and what, ideally, you would like to happen. You are going to close the gap between where you are and where you want to be.

- If you were writing your own script, what would you do?
- What would you be saying?
- How would you be feeling?
- What would be the desired outcome?

Imagine you're playing a video of your tantrum in your head. Press pause. When the picture starts again, imagine what you would like to happen in an ideal situation, with you feeling calm and in control.

In order to tackle this particular hotspot, complete the Parent Tantrum Action Wheel opposite. Make a list of all the things that you can do that will help you to keep calm and in control the next time this situation occurs. Aim to close the gap between where you are now and where you want to be. Put one idea in each segment of the wheel. Remember, it must be something that you can do, something that is within your control – not theirs.

One of my mums, Keisha, broke down when she talked to me about the way she was shouting at her children in the mornings. She had a son of five years and a daughter who was three years old. Keisha was devastated

PARENT TANTRUM ACTION

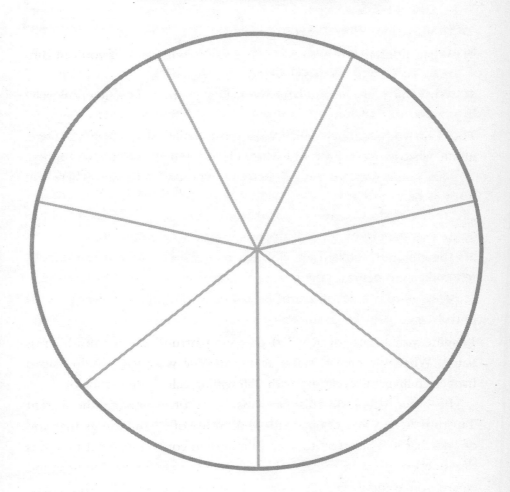

by the way she was behaving. The children were arriving at school unhappy and Keisha was getting to work in a state of total stress. She wrote down her schedule of exactly what she wanted to happen in the mornings before everyone left the house. Then she completed the Tantrum Action Wheel – even though she insisted at first that she had absolutely no idea what she could do to make things better.

In fact, Keisha selected just three simple ideas from her Parent Tantrum Action Wheel that transformed her mornings. Firstly, she decide to get up 10 minutes earlier each day so that she could have a cup of tea in peace and focus on being positive, rather than 'hitting the ground running' when the alarm went off. Secondly, she decided to get the children up 15 minutes earlier each day. She had wanted them to have as long a sleep as possible but this was making their 'getting ready' time so short it was stressful for them all. Thirdly, instead of having the TV on while they were getting dressed and having breakfast, she decided to use it as an incentive. The children were only allowed to watch TV once they had dressed and eaten. It wasn't just on. This helped Keisha to establish the morning schedule she was so desperate for. It also meant that the children watched less TV, but they didn't realise because they were so keen to get everything done first so that they could switch it on!

Brainstorm as many different ideas as you can think of to help keep control when you feel a tantrum coming on. Think of everything you possibly can. Choose just one thing on your list that you can try. It can be a big change or a small one. If you keep on doing what you're doing, you'll keep on getting what you're getting.

Once you have completed the Parent Tantrum Action Wheel, rank your ideas from one to seven with number one being the action you'd like to try first.

1. _____

2. _____

3. _____

4. _____

5. _____

6. _____

7. _____

Action

You have now come up with seven actions you can take that will help you get a little closer to your ideal scenario. These are ideas that will help you to stay calm, keep control and be the parent you want to be.

Put one idea into your diary for every day next week and be sure to put them into effect.

Today, when you're faced with your daily parent tantrum hotspot, commit to doing at least one thing differently. If you keep on doing what you're doing, you'll keep on getting what you're getting.

You have come up with seven great ideas. You're the expert on your own family situation. Take it a step at a time. Give each idea a go and in just one week you will see a significant difference.

DAY 7:
PARENT TANTRUM UPDATE

Look back at the table that you filled in at the beginning of the chapter giving the Top Six Parent Tantrum Signs.

At the beginning of the week, you filled in how often you were experiencing those parent tantrum signs.

Look at each item on the list in turn. If, during the course of this week, you feel you have made positive steps forward in this area, give yourself a tick.

It doesn't matter if you think you still have a long way to go to get to where you want to be. What is important is that you are moving in the right direction. If you take small steps, you can get there.

TOP SIX PARENT TANTRUM SIGNS	POSITIVE IMPROVEMENT
1. You experience negative feelings about yourself as a parent, including lack of confidence, guilt, anger, sadness and regret.	
2. You shout or raise your voice, saying critical or negative things to your children that you would not say if calm.	
3. You experience negative feelings towards your children and blame them for your loss of control.	
4. You pay negative attention to your children and it usually involves 'telling off'.	
5. You lose control and start acting your children's age and not your own.	
6. You feel signs of physical stress and tension.	

■ Have you managed to move forward in any parent tantrum areas?
■ How does that feel?
■ What difference has it made to you and to your family life this week?

You have now reached day seven of your action plan. By completing each of the daily exercises you will have come a long way in establishing a strategy that will help you to tame your parent tantrums – and keep control even when your children are losing theirs.

By now you have:

■ Spotted your own parent tantrum signs.
■ Raised your game to be the parent you want to be.

■ Given tantrum words the 'red card'.

■ Re-framed challenging situations and started seeing the children you love.

■ Started playing the game by your rules – not theirs.

■ Taken action to deal with parent tantrum hotspots.

Think about how you felt at the beginning of the week and how you feel today.

■ What has been the biggest challenge for you this week?

■ What is the biggest positive difference in the way you feel today compared with the feelings you experienced at the beginning of the week?

■ How does it feel to have developed a positive strategy full of effective alternatives to shouting and other everyday parent tantrums?

■ How much closer do you feel to being the parent you want to be?

Action

Read your Parent Achievement Log (see page 291) for this week and recognise all that you have accomplished. Take your time and enjoy the feeling of achievement. Focus on the difference you are making to yourself and to your family by thinking and acting positively and taking control.

Now rank your achievements from one to seven with number one being the achievement that has had the biggest impact on you and your family this week.

1. _____

2. _____

3. _____

4. _____

5. _____

6. _____

7. _____

■ What makes this your biggest achievement of the week?

■ What impact has it had on you?

■ What impact has it had on your children?

■ How does that feel?

chapter six

communicating with children

who don't listen but hear everything you say about them

One of the commonest complaints among the parents I coach is that their children just don't listen to what they are saying. When I ask the parents what makes them so sure, they usually say that they know that's the case because their children don't do as they are told. If they were listening, they would.

Take a look at this extract from a conversation that a client of mine, Hannah, had with her son Jack, who's nearly three years old. As you are reading it, imagine that you are Jack. What message is he getting from his mum?

Jack: Mum, will you help me to colour this?

Mum: Yes, in a minute

Jack: Can you help me colour this now?

Mum: What do you need me for? You can do it. I told you I will later on.

Jack: Please Mum can you help?

Mum: Jack, I've told you I will when I've finished this.

Jack: Will you do this bit yellow?

Mum: Stop asking me the same thing over and over again. Why don't you ever listen to what I say?

Jack: Please Mum.

Mum: If you keep going on at me I'll never get this finished.

Jack: Please Mum, can we do it now?

Mum: That's it. No. I'm not going to do it. I just wish you would do what
        you're told. Just go and do something by yourself.

What did you think as you were reading it? What message did Hannah think she was sending to Jack? What did Jack hear? What caused the communication to break down? In just a few minutes, a simple request deteriorated into a heated exchange.

Once we'd listened to this recording, I asked Hannah what three things she could do differently next time, if a similar situation arose, instead of getting rattled with Jack. Here are her suggestions:

1. 'I can understand why Jack's feeling a little confused. I start off by saying I'll help him "in a minute". That soon became, "later" and then, "when I've finished". He lives in the "now" and I usually live in the "later"! I had my mind on other things and I wasn't sending him a clear message.'
2. 'I would have felt less stressed if we'd been in the same room. Jack was in the TV room and I was in the kitchen sorting out the washing. The fact that we were shouting at each other was stressful.'
3. 'I feel bad that, in the end, I get cross with Jack. Listening to the tape makes me realise that all he really wants to do is spend time with me. And I love spending time with him. I always have loads to do but I want to tell him that I do have time for him.'

This was a very helpful evaluation. The message Hannah was communicating wasn't clear. It wasn't that Jack wasn't listening, but that Mum wasn't saying what she meant – and didn't mean what she said. Her point about being in the same room is a good one. We can easily fall into the habit of communicating with each other from different rooms – and sometimes different floors in the house. Raising the volume – yours and your children's – can raise stress levels, so make every effort to be in the same place when you are communicating. Hannah is successful in seeing the scene through Jack's eyes. He's not being difficult, he just wants his mum's attention because he wants to spend time with her.

I'm sure Hannah's experience and feedback will strike a chord with you.

The way we communicate – verbally and non-verbally – with our children is absolutely vital. This week, we are going to look at practical ways for you to boost your skills in this area. Communication is one area where you can make positive changes straight away, so I know you'll notice the difference from day one. Many of the parents I work with also find that their newly-acquired skills impact positively on all their relationships – with friends, relatives and colleagues.

The key to effective communication lies with you. As you'll appreciate, you can make changes in you and these will impact on your relationship with your children. Rather than focusing on what your children aren't doing, we will focus on more effective ways to communicate what you want them to do.

It's also important to acknowledge that while many children **don't listen** – they **still hear** everything you have to say about them. This week, I want you to be very clear that even when your children appear to be ignoring you by not listening, they may actually be hearing everything you say about them. Any negative messages you send will impact negatively on them. Any positive messages you send will impact positively on them. The decision is yours.

This week I want you to focus on exactly what you say to and about your children and make a great effort to stop any negative comments leaving your lips.

Not only will this be a great exercise for you, but it will also have a significant influence on how your children learn to communicate. Effective communication skills will be picked up from you and this is an invaluable skill that will help them throughout their lives. Think about how you respond to other people. If they are positive with you, you are likely to respond in a similar way. If they are negative with you, you are likely to respond in a negative way. Your children will take their lead from you.

Remember that the key to reducing stress and boosting energy is being positive in thought and deed. By teaching your children to communicate positively, you are building a vital foundation for their future lives. You can help them to live their lives positively and to communicate that positive energy to everyone they come into contact with. Just take a few minutes now, to listen to your children.

- What kinds of things do they say that are positive?
- What kinds of things do they say that are negative?
- Is their language predominantly positive or negative?
- How large a gap is there between where they are now and where you want them to be?

By improving your skills, you can help them make a big leap forward.

On a scale of 1 to 10, how would you rate your communication skills with your children? A rating of 10 indicates excellent skills. A rating of 1 indicates that there are a lot of positive changes you could make. Circle the number that applies to you.

1   2   3   4   5   6   7   8   9   10

Take a look at the communication skills listed in the Communication Wheel opposite.

- Which of these communication skills would you say you are best at?
- What is your particular strength in that area?
- Which of these communication skills would you say is your least effective?
- What is the main reason for that?
- If you could boost your communication skills in one area, which one would you choose to begin with?
- What impact would that make on your relationship with your children?

We're going to take positive action in all seven of these communication skills this week. By making small changes, we can make a big difference.

COMMUNICATION

Action

The key to all good, stress-free communication is talking positively, so today really focus on boosting this skill. This skill is important all the time. You may be in the habit of using negative language without even realising it, so listen carefully to see if you can catch yourself being negative in any way.

Today, use positive language not negative language. When other parents ask how you're feeling, tell them only about all the good things in your life. Even if they use negative language with you, use positive language with them. It may take a little practice.

When they ask you how your children are doing, tell them about all the great things – the smiles, the fun – and not the sleepless nights or the tantrums. The choice is yours.

When you ask your children to do something, explain the benefits of doing it – rather than the consequences of not doing it.

Keep a record over the next 24 hours. Focus on getting through the day talking as positively as you can. You will notice a difference, not just in what you are saying but also in how you are feeling. By talking positively instead of negatively, you are creating a positive frame of mind that will impact on the way you feel – and I'm confident that you'll notice a change in your children too.

It's really important that we acknowledge our achievements as parents. Each day I want you to make a note of your biggest achievement (see Parent Achievement Log, page 291). It may be something you achieve when you're carrying out your daily coaching action. Or it may be something that just happens in the course of the day and you think to yourself, 'Yes! That was great!' You decide what is significant for you.

DAY 2: WHO CONTROLS THE TV ZAPPER? CUT DOWN THE INTERFERENCE

Today is going to be a significant day in your week. All the parents I have worked with on these exercises tell me that it has made a huge difference in their homes.

If you want to talk with your children and maximise the impact of your words, you need to create the optimum environment. The noise threshold in many homes is extremely high. We live in a multi-media age and we've become accustomed to having all sorts of noises going on all the time. Parents often say to me that children don't come with a volume control. But it's hardly surprising, given the amount of noise they compete with at home on a daily basis. It creeps up and up until it becomes unbearable.

When mums and dads talk about what causes their stress, noise is one of the commonest factors cited. The trouble is that everyone just gets louder and louder to make themselves heard and the noise problem is exacerbated.

Today, I want you to focus on positive changes that you can make to help reduce noise levels in your home – avoid anything that might interfere with your communication with your children and get back in touch with the fun of just talking.

Let's take the prime culprit in many homes, the TV. I want you to take your time in answering the following questions:

- Who controls the TV remote control in your house?
- Who do you want to control the TV remote control in your house?
- How many hours of TV or video do your children watch daily?
- How many hours of TV or video would you like them to watch daily?

Think hard about your answer to the last question. Parents will often say that their children watch too much TV, but they have no clear idea how much, in an ideal world, they would like them to watch. If you do not know what goal you are aiming for, you are very unlikely to achieve it. Be specific about the amount of time in hours/minutes that you feel happy about letting your child spend in front of the TV. Now think about your own TV viewing habits.

- How many hours of TV do you watch daily?
- How often is the TV on in the background, when no one is really watching it?
- What message are you sending to your children about the important part the TV has in the family home?

Many of the parents I coach say that they think their children watch too much TV – but they don't feel up to tackling the problem because of the arguments this causes.

I'm not anti-television. In fact, I believe that it can play a positive role in the home. TV can be a positive or negative influence. The key questions are who is in control, and how is it being watched? In most homes, the children, not the parents control the TV remote. Lots of mums and dads have just got into the habit of letting their little ones watch lots of TV, and there can be major tantrums if parents try to switch it off.

One of the mums I was working with, Sian, said that when she thought about the questions above, they were a real eye-opener. She worked out that her two-year-old, Remi, was watching up to four hours of TV daily. When I asked Sian what stopped her from switching it off, she said that it's often easier to have the TV on, especially when she's trying to get things done in the home. Sian realised that she needed to change her approach, rather than moaning at Remi for watching TV all the time. By letting Remi get his own way, she was sending him the message that the TV is the most important thing in the house.

Sian also realised that she could be setting a much more positive example herself. She often had the TV on, without actually watching it, when she was doing other things. She'd just got used to having background noise.

Sian's goal was to cut Remi's TV initially from four hours to three hours daily, and then gradually reduce it even more. She was specific in what she wanted to achieve in one week – a reduction of one hour daily.

Think about the TV in your home. How much of a reduction on the TV time would you like to make on a daily basis?

In the Alternatives To TV Wheel on page 133, I want you to list all the things that you could do with your children instead of letting them watch the TV or videos.

I want you to think about all the fun that you could have with them. Here's Sian's wheel:

Sian said she found this helpful because it made her realise how much the family had slipped into the habit of watching TV – when they could be having a lot more fun.

In fact, Sian succeeded in cutting Remi's TV viewing by 50 per cent – and they've both thoroughly enjoyed the time they've spent together. Usually, Sian would let Remi watch TV while she did her jobs. Now Remi helps her sort the washing and cook.

They've been out together more than usual. Sian's started taking him with her when she drops off her five-year-old, Ali, at school instead of leaving Remi at home watching TV with her husband. It means that Remi can play with the other toddlers and it has made him much more confident.

Sian admitted that it means she has to be much more organised – but she said that this was great. She successfully rearranged the bath times and made them longer. Instead of viewing bath time as a bit of a chore that had to be done, Sian has started to think of it as fun.

Sian has also decided to use the TV positively, as an incentive, and said her best decision was to stop them watching it just before bed time. With no arguments about switching the TV off, this has made bed times much easier.

Action

Your action for today is a very simple one. Switch off the TV and keep it off – all day. Pressing that one small button will make a huge difference. Yes, I want you to go for a full 24 hours without the TV on in your home. This may be a great challenge for you because TV has become such a habit, but I know you can do this if you're really committed. That means a TV-free zone for you and all the family.

Now complete your own Alternatives To TV Wheel opposite.

Once you have done it, take a look at all the ideas you have there and rank them from one to seven with number one being the idea you would like to try first. Every day this week, I want you to put into practice one of those ideas – at a time when your children would normally be watching TV.

Just try one idea a day, and gradually move through your list.

Take a look at your Alternatives to TV Wheel and decide how you want to spend the time with your children today. Enjoy yourselves.

ALTERNATIVES TO TV

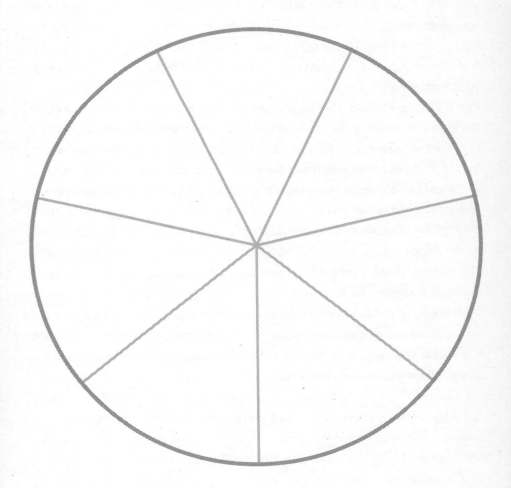

DAY 3: LOOK WHO'S TALKING – LEARN TO LISTEN

The next step is to focus on how much time you spend listening to your children, and how much time they spend listening to you. In most family homes, the majority of parents spend about 90 per cent of the time talking and 10 per cent of the time listening. One major way of improving communication with your little ones is to reverse those percentages. Focus on spending 10 per cent of your time talking and 90 per cent listening. You will probably be very surprised by the results. Just by listening to what our children have to say, you may identify positive changes you'd like to make in what you're doing as a parent. Your children won't be backward in coming forward to tell you what they want and how they feel. Just imagine how much you can learn from them and how much better you'll get to know them over the course of today.

It's also important to ensure that when you say you are listening, you really are. We've all assured our children that we're hanging on their every word. But we both know that isn't the case. We might want to, but we let other things get in the way. We may be sorting the laundry, talking on the phone, writing a birthday card, packing nursery lunch or working through our mental 'to do' list. We say we're listening and we're not! In my experience, children know when you are and when you are not listening. Just think about it from their point of view. How would you feel if someone told you they were listening to you – but you knew categorically that they were not?

How do you feel when someone takes the trouble to give you their full attention? By listening to your child, you are sending them the clear message that you value what they say – and also that you value them. One of my clients, Jan, found it very helpful to 'listen' with her eyes first and then her ears. By looking at her child, they both knew that Jan was paying attention and ready to listen to what Tom had to say.

■ How would you rate your skill at listening to your children?
Poor   OK   Good   Very Good   Excellent
■ What one thing could you do to improve it?

Action

Today, I want you to listen with your eyes, your ears – and with your heart – to everything you're being told. Remember, the target is to listen for 90 per cent of the time and talk for 10 per cent. You can do it, if you really want to.

I want you to spend as much time as possible listening at child-level. Whenever you are spending time with your little ones, get down on your hands and knees or do whatever you have to do to communicate at their level.

It's often the case that we may pick up our children to give them a cuddle – and bring them up to our eye-level – but for most of the time we're giants in their world. This is your opportunity to establish real rapport with them, and have lots of fun doing it. It can be great to see the world through a child's eyes again!

DAY 4:
ASKING THE RIGHT QUESTIONS

The key to good communication is to ask the right questions. As a parent, you can have a significant impact on the development of your children's mental skills just by focusing on asking creative, 'open' questions.

If you ask good quality questions, you will boost the quality of your children's thought processes and answers and significantly improve their ability to communicate. The best questions to use are 'open' questions rather than 'closed' questions. A 'closed' question allows children to give a simple 'yes' or 'no' answer. 'Yes' or 'no' answers close doors. An 'open' question requires children to give a descriptive answer and promotes self-awareness.

One of my clients, Catherine, was worried that her three-year-old, Calum, wasn't talking very much. When she spent time with him, he never seemed to be interested in chatting or have much to say.

Catherine is a journalist and so is used to asking questions. So it came as a real eye-opener to her when she identified her questioning technique as a key area ripe for improvement.

Over the course of one day, she recorded the conversations she had with Calum and then played them back, making a note of the words she used when she asked him a question.

She was quite shocked to discover that the word she used most of all when talking to Calum was, 'Why?' It was one of his favourites, too, and Catherine's tone of voice changed when she answered him. Taping her conversations was Catherine's idea – and it was an excellent one. It meant she could really take stock of her conversations with Calum and think about how she could improve her performance – and his.

I asked Catherine what it was about the 'Why?' question that made it so negative. She said that she didn't like being asked 'Why' questions herself, as they made her feel defensive. They seemed to have the same effect on Calum. He felt he was being put on the spot and having to justify what he was doing. That was just how she felt when people asked her, 'Why?'

Listening to the tape made it quite clear to her that Calum wasn't talking much because she wasn't asking the right questions to get him talking. I asked her to make a list of all of the words she could use instead of 'Why?' that would provide a positive opportunity for Calum to talk more.

Catherine's list looked like this

■ How ...?
■ What ...?
■ When ...?
■ Who ...?
■ How much ...?
■ How many ...?
■ Imagine ...
■ Where ...?
■ If ...

Catherine decided to write these words on yellow sticky notes and put them around the house – to remind her to use them every time she talked with Calum. Within seven days, she reported a dramatic improvement in the quality and length of their conversations. Not only was he talking more and becoming much more engaged with Catherine, but his vocabulary seemed to have taken a huge leap forward. He was using words that

Catherine had never heard him say before, and didn't think he knew. Perhaps it was just that she hadn't been asking the right questions before. Catherine also noticed that Calum was beginning to use her question words when asking his own questions – instead of his favourite, 'Why?'

I want you to complete the same exercise as Catherine. What is the key word or phrase that you keep using when you're asking your children questions – but that you'd like to cut from your vocabularly? Make a list of more effective words or phrases that you could use instead.

Action

Today, I want you to concentrate on asking 'open' and creative questions when you are talking to your children. Whenever you are asking questions, focus on what you are saying and how you are saying it. Think about the best possible way to get the best quality answer from your little one. Put the list of words you would like to use in a visible place so that you are constantly reminded. Now, focus on using one word from your list every time you're tempted to ask a 'closed' or limiting question.

The first time you do this, you may find you have to make a conscious effort. But the more you do it, the easier it becomes. You may be breaking the habit of asking closed questions that has become established over many years. Be positive, this habit can be broken – with great results for you and your children.

Work hard today at making sure you do not use 'Why?' when you talk to your child.

DAY 5: SAY WHAT YOU MEAN AND MEAN WHAT YOU SAY

The next step is to focus on saying what you mean – and meaning what you say – when you are talking to your children.

Firstly, it is important that you say what you mean and that you are very clear about the message you are sending to your children. In the excerpt at the beginning of the chapter, Hannah was sending all sorts of mixed messages to her son that left him confused and her irritated.

One of the most effective ways of producing a clear message is to focus on being very specific when you are talking to your children. We tend to talk to them in very general terms in normal conversation, but you and your children will find it helpful to get into the habit of being as precise as possible.

Let's use the example at the beginning of this chapter. What was it that Hannah was trying to say to her son Jack? She started off by saying she would help Jack, 'in a minute'. That soon became, 'later' and then, 'when I've finished this'. The message she was communicating was not clear. It wasn't that Jack wasn't listening, it was that Mum wasn't saying what she meant – and didn't mean what she said.

The concept of time can often lead to confusion in a little one's mind. How often do you say, 'I'll do it in a minute', when what you actually mean is quite different. Don't say things as a delaying tactic. Think about what you really mean and say it.

One of my clients, Elaine, was exasperated because her children would never tidy up their toys and so the whole house was in a constant mess. She'd repeatedly tell them to tidy up – but never see a visible difference.

At one of her coaching sessions, I asked her what words she used. She told me, 'Tidy up your toys' or 'tidy up your bedroom'. I asked her what she could say instead that might have a positive effect and bring about her desired outcome. She only had to think about it for a minute or two before she came up with her own answer. Instead of telling them what to do she was going to ask them, and explain in a positive way the reason for doing it. Elaine identified that, because this issue was stressful for her, her tone was always negative and nagging. She also recognised that her idea of a 'tidy' room or 'tidy' toys might be quite different from theirs. Perhaps they thought they were doing a good job, whereas she thought they were being deliberately difficult and disobedient.

She decided to give each of them extremely specific tasks, breaking down the big picture into small, achievable targets. Instead of saying, 'Tidy up' she said, 'Tom, can you put the pieces of jigsaw into the box so that they don't get lost.' She asked them to do particular jobs, one at a time. She set clear goals that both she and the children understood. She was very impressed with the results and they responded well to being praised instead of nagged. Elaine recognised that this process took longer, but it was more fun – and certainly more effective. She decided to start the tidying up process earlier than before and to make it all part of the game. Both she and the children started to enjoy the challenge of keeping the home tidy and they even came up with their own ideas about what they could do to help. They had great fun establishing a toy box system with picture labels that the children drew and coloured.

As well as saying what you mean, it is vital that you mean what you say. Some of the most serious communication breakdowns come about because parents give their children inconsistent messages. Sometimes parents are not even aware they are doing it. Sometimes they just do it because it suits them in the short term.

The biggest culprits are the 'idle threat' or the 'unfulfilled promise'.

THE IDLE THREAT

How often do you make an idle threat to your toddler? Many of the mums and dads I coach identify this as a key problem area. In the heat of the moment, they'll threaten something to get their children to do as they're told – but if their children refuse the parents never carry out the threat.

One mum, Aziza, was constantly using threats when communicating with her toddler. Every time there was a stand-off, she would threaten to take one of his toys away or not let him watch his favourite video, or not take him out. But when push came to shove, Aziza never carried out the threats. She would repeat the threats again and again, but then feel guilty and let her toddler do what he wanted to do anyway. The message Aziza was sending was very clear: 'I'm making a fuss but I'm not going to do anything about it.' So, if you were her son, what would you do?

THE UNFULFILLED PROMISE

The other big problem area is the unfulfilled promise. Many of my clients confess to promising things to their children if they do something, but then failing to keep the promise. They will offer some treat in the heat of the moment to make their children behave in a certain way, but often have absolutely no intention of providing it because they don't have the time or the money. They hope that their children will forget, but of course they rarely do.

Think about how you communicate with your children. Would you say that you are more inclined to make idle threats or unfulfilled promises? How does that make you feel?

Action

Today, instead of telling your children what to do, ask them to do it and explain the reason for asking them. Focus on keeping a positive frame of mind and tone of voice. Be as specific as you can in all your instructions. Set your children clear goals so that you and they will know when these have been achieved. This will have a significant impact on communication and build your children's confidence.

Focus on getting through the whole day without making one idle threat or one unfulfilled promise. Approach challenging situations calmly. Tears and tantrums occur when communication breaks down and you start to act your children's age – not your own.

DAY 6:
POSITIVE TALK TIME

The next stage is to focus on creating 'positive talk time'.

Over the past week how often have you had some positive talk time with (not to) your children? By that, I mean actually sat down and talked with your children and given them your undivided attention.

- How did it feel?
- How did they respond?

Talk time doesn't have to last for hours to have an impact. You need to focus on quality and giving your children your full attention. We all talk to our children a lot don't we? More often than not, we'll be multi-tasking – talking to them about the game they are playing, while we simultaneously wash up, sort the laundry, write a shopping list, pack a school lunch and answer the telephone.

There's often so little time and so much to do that we can get through whole days without giving our children just a few minutes of undivided attention. But a few minutes of full attention can mean the world to your children – and to you.

One of my clients, Ingrid, said that she was always so busy that she never really sat down with three-year-old, Rachel, and talked with her. Rachel was always around and they chatted, but Ingrid was always busy doing 101 other things.

I asked her to complete a Talk-time Wheel, identifying the key times when she had opportunities to talk to Rachel. This included occasions such as taking Rachel to the nursery, meal times, bath time and bed time. Ingrid's problem was that she always felt that she was rushing. Even at these key times with Rachel she was busy doing lots of things at once. When she was walking Rachel to the nursery, Ingrid would be thinking about all the jobs she had to do during the day once she'd dropped Rachel off. When Rachel was eating her tea, Ingrid would be talking to her while she loaded the dishwasher or ironed. When Rachel was having a bath, Ingrid would be sorting out laundry or tidying the bathroom. When it was bed time, Rachel was keen to chat but Ingrid was usually tired and just wanted Rachel to get to sleep.

Ingrid identified meal times as the priority area she wanted to work on. For one whole week, she would sit down with Rachel when she was having her tea and talk with her. She said this was difficult to begin with as she was surrounded by lots of things that needed doing. But once she'd committed to it – she loved it.

Ingrid put jobs out of her mind and just enjoyed talking with Rachel. It was just 30 minutes in a day but she had created quality talk time. Ingrid was very pleased with the results. Not only did she get the opportunity for a proper chat, she felt more relaxed herself as she was not constantly on the move. Rachel's response was good too. She began to eat lots of food that she'd previously just played with because Mum was there to give her attention and make meal times fun.

Ingrid decided to switch on the telephone answering maching during this time. She'd been in the habit of picking up the phone whenever friends called. Now she wanted to create some uninterrupted peace.

Action

Complete the Talk-time Wheel opposite. Identify the times when you have the opportunity to create undisturbed talk time with your children. You now have seven great ideas that you can integrate into your everyday life. You can decide how long you want talk time to be. Time is an issue for all parents but remember that every minute is valuable, and the question of how much time you spend is yours.

Decide when you want to book your talk time into your diary and put one idea in for every day this week. Commit to making it happen. There are always lots of reasons for it not to happen – but focus on the reason to make it happen today. It's the most important date in your diary – so make sure you keep it.

How much do you know about your children, about what they think and how they feel?

Make a list of the top three questions you'd like to know the answers to. This is a real opportunity for you to get to know your children and for them to get to know you too!

1. _____

2. _____

3. _____

TALK TIME

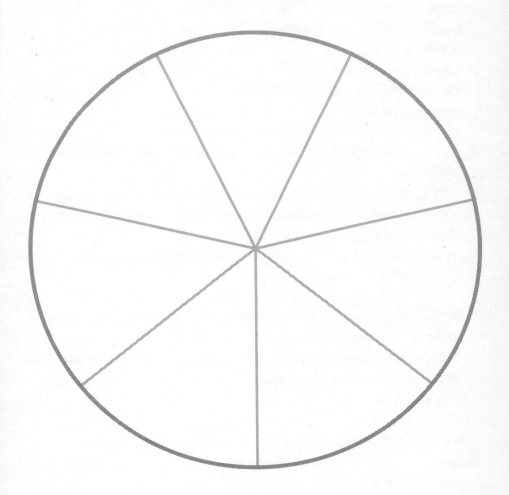

DAY 7:
COMMUNICATION UPDATE

So now we are at the end of your week of boosting communication skills.

Take another look at the list below. By following the 7-day action plan, you have made positive changes in all of these areas. You have now reached day seven of your action plan. By completing each of the daily exercises you will have come a long way in establishing a strategy that will help you to communicate even more effectively with your children and everyone else around you. You're also providing a great communication role model for your child.

By now you have:

- Committed to talking positively – not just to your children, but to everyone.
- Cut down interference.
- Developed an active listening strategy.
- Boosted your 'open' question skills.
- Focused on saying what you mean and meaning what you say.
- Created positive 'talk time'.

- Which of the communication skills have you most enjoyed working on over the past week?
- What positive impact has this had on your relationship with your children?
- What differences do you notice in the way your children communicate with you?

Take a look back at the communication skills rating you gave yourself at the beginning of the week. If you have followed the 7-day action plan, you will have noticed significant changes. Think about how you felt at the beginning of the week and how you feel today.

- What has been the biggest challenge for you this week?
- What is the biggest positive difference in the way you feel today compared with the feelings you experienced at the beginning of the week?

Action

Read your Parent Achievement Log (see page 291) for this week and recognise all that you have achieved. Good communication is vital for family health and you have made effective progress. Take your time and enjoy the feeling of achievement. Focus on the difference you are making to yourself and to your family by thinking and acting positively and taking control of the way that you communicate with your child. You're sending positive messages to your children who may still have work to do 'listening' – but are hearing everything positive you say about them. Now rank your achievements from one to seven with number one being the achievement that has had the biggest impact on you and your family this week.

1. _____

2. _____

3. _____

4. _____

5. _____

6. _____

7. _____

- What makes this your biggest achievement of the week?
- What impact has it had on you?
- What impact has it had on your relationship with your children?
- How does that feel?

Focus on your children's communication skills today and spend time talking to them about what they do well. Over the past week, they will have picked up many of the things that you are working on – you are their role model. Praise them when they use good communication skills. Catch them 'red-handed' at being good communicators.

chapter seven

stop worrying and start living

In this chapter, we are going to focus on what parents worry about and make positive moves forward to reduce the levels of anxiety that you may feel in your life. Many people say that they feel more anxious after having a family.

Here are some letters I received recently from parents desperate to do something about their high anxiety levels. Their concerns are extremely common ones.

Katy: 'I have a three-year-old son, Tom, who's very happy and healthy. But since he was born, I find myself worrying that something will happen to him. It's not just his safety. I worry that he will be taken away from me. My beautiful little boy. I also worry about myself and my partner dying and leaving him an orphan. I was 40 when he was born and as an older mum I really worry a lot about what's going to happen in the future. I get frightened by all the stories in the press, especially about breast cancer, and am terrified of getting it. I used to be such a positive person – I just can't understand what's happened to me. My partner, Ben, is very understanding but he thinks I worry unnecessarily a lot of the time.'

Ram: 'My wife and I have two toddlers and another child on the way. I just love being a dad and it's really made me re-think my priorities. It's hard to put into words what a difference having a family has made to me. I also have a challenging job that I enjoy. But I have one major problem, I have this overwhelming anxiety about my health and fear that I will die young. My dad had a history of heart problems and I worry that I have inherited this. On top of that – and I don't know why I do this – but I smoke. I've tried to give it up but I just can't resist a cigarette in social situations and a lot of our friends smoke. I only have cigarettes now and again – and never in the house, as I go into the garden – but I can't give up and it just makes me worry more and more about my health. What can I do? The worry I feel takes away the enjoyment I want to feel about being a dad. It sounds ridiculous, but worrying about dying dominates my thoughts and often spoils family times because I start imagining all sorts of awful things that might happen. Sometimes it's so bad I just take myself off to bed and won't talk to anyone. They can't help the way I feel.'

Shakti: 'I can't stop worrying about everything. It sounds silly but it's driving me mad. You name it and I worry about it: shopping, finding a parking space, the house being a mess, my divorce, how I'm going to find the money for a party for Zachary. In my worst moments, I worry about would happen to him if I wasn't around. No matter how hard I try, I go to bed worrying about a whole list of things and it often keeps me awake for hours.'

Katy, Ram and Shakti's experiences are typical. Parents' anxieties often manifest themselves in concerns about their own health and mortality or their children's – and often both. Many parents also report experiences similar to Shakti's. She's become a constant worrier and there's always something she feels anxious about.

The important point to recognise is that these feelings of anxiety are entirely natural. The transformation from just being you to being a mum or dad is huge. Being responsible for yourself is one thing but being responsible for a little one who is totally dependent on you is significantly different. The reason you feel anxious is because you are taking your responsibilities seriously – and that just shows what a great parent you are. It is also positive to focus on issues such as health, as this is a key area for you and your family. We need to get to the point where you are focusing on these issues in a very positive way. This will help to reduce the stress you feel and boost your energy so that you can get on and enjoy being a parent again.

The problem here is that your anxiety gets in the way of your enjoying family life – and that is not positive. If you are focusing on illness rather than good health, this has a powerful negative impact. Anxiety is an incredibly powerful emotion. As well as worrying about major issues such as death, you also start to experience increased anxiety about other smaller, everyday family things. Many of the parents I work with say that they worry about so many things now that they have children – and not just issues related to the family. Issues that they would have dealt with in their stride before having children now seem major obstacles to be overcome. An everyday challenge becomes a crisis. This is a key area and one that you want to do something about – and quickly. Once you begin to make positive changes in this area, you should notice a difference in your stress levels immediately.

The problem is that the more time you spend thinking about issues that worry you, the more anxious you become. The actual process of worrying does absolutely nothing to change the situation or move you forward. Instead of making you feel better, it makes you feel worse. Instead of wasting time on negative thoughts, you want to be investing time in positive action to address the issues that concern you. This will have a positive impact in every area of your life.

Over the next seven days, you and I are going to tackle the 'anxiety gremlin' together. I know that if you commit to the action plan you will make positive steps forward and be in a different place by this time next week. Worry is an intense feeling that has the power to dominate you in a very negative way. You give it that power, so start today to take control again. The good news is that feelings of anxiety are created within you, so this means that you can take practical steps to reduce their power over you.

This will increase your energy levels. It also means that you will make big strides forward as a role model for your children. If they see you looking anxious, worrying all of the time and talking about being worried, they'll absorb the message that this is what life is like. If they see you taking practical steps to deal with issues that concern you and rising to the challenges that worry you, they'll grow up knowing that finding solutions is more fun than dwelling on problems.

On a scale of 1 to 10, indicate your current level of anxiety. A score of 1 indicates a low level of anxiety and a score of 10 an extremely high level of anxiety. Circle the number below that best reflects the way you feel.

1   2   3   4   5   6   7   8   9   10

The score you award is subjective. Whatever you have scored means that there will always be some room for improvement.

Focus on your feeling of anxiety when it is at its most powerful.

- What impact does it have on you?
- How would you describe the feeling?
- What negative impact does feeling anxious have on you and family life?
- What does it stop you from doing or enjoying?
- What is the cost to you and to family life of your feeling anxious?

Today is the day when you are going to face up to everything that is making you feel anxious at the moment. These may be major issues – such as anxiety over your health or your children's health. Or they may be smaller, niggling worries that you haven't addressed, perhaps because you feel you can't face them at the moment, or you haven't got around to doing anything about them. Today you will get to grips with your anxieties and begin to move forward.

Just to give you an idea, here is the worry list that Katy completed.

Katy's Worry List

- Getting up early to get Ben to the station.
- Tom doesn't seem himself – quiet.
- Saw paper headlines – breast cancer – scared me.
- Mum phoned. Elderly. Worry that don't see her enough and she's lonely.
- Put phone down and think about Mum not being around to call me every day.
- Need to find Tom a nursery but sure all have waiting lists. Left it too late.
- Think about me being ill. What would happen then?
- Post came. Bill for phone bigger than expected.

- Worried about our finances generally. Now I'm not working, money is tight.
- Can't talk to Ben about money as he's under pressure at work
- If Tom's not at nursery, how can I earn some money to help out?
- Need to buy birthday present for Alice but won't have car to get to shops.
- Poured with rain last night. Roof leaking a little. Need to look at it.
- Best friend Anne called. Wanted to talk but I had so much to do.
- Tom's going to play with Anne and her boys later. Will be in the park. Worry about him there. How will Anne cope with three toddlers? Will she see him all the time? He's started running off to play hide and seek. Dangerous.
- Hear radio story about cancer scares and children's food. Turn off.
- Empty bins. Ben had quite a bit to drink last night. He's stressed and putting on weight. Want him to be healthy and happy.
- Tom's watching same video again. Worry I'm letting him down.
- Tom isn't interested in using toilet. I just can't get him trained.

It may or may not surprise you to know that this is Katy's list from 7am to 10am. Just three hours worth of worries! It got much longer as the day went on. She was really surprised to see the length of the list – no wonder she wasn't sleeping very well. She said that it was shocking to see so many worries listed like that but it helped her to see them in writing. She felt that by putting them down in black and white she was taking the first step in wrestling back control.

Action

Today I want you to complete your own Worry List. Keep a diary of every-thing you feel anxious about. It doesn't matter how small the worry may seem to you, if it pops into your head, include it in the list. Make it easy for yourself to keep adding to the list. Have pieces of paper on the fridge door or anywhere else accessible around the house. Keep paper with you wherever you go. As soon as you begin to feel worried about something, add it to the list. Be as specific as you can about the cause of the worry.

It is very important that you write each worry down because then you can deal with it. Once you have your list in black and white you can start to take positive actions to address the worries instead of wasting time just thinking about them. Write your worries down as they occur to you, don't think you'll remember them and write the list later.

Once you have completed your list, take a good look at it.

■ What is your single biggest reason for wanting to reduce the levels of anxiety in your life?

■ What impact will it have on you and your relationship with your family?

It's really important that we acknowledge our achievements as parents. Each day I want you to make a note of your biggest achievement (see Parent Achievement Log, page 291). It may be something you achieve when you're carrying out your daily coaching action. Or it may be something that just happens in the course of the day and you think to yourself, 'Yes! That was great!' You decide what is significant for you.

DAY 2: CHANNEL YOUR ENERGY IN A POSITIVE WAY

The key to reducing the impact of worry on your life and reducing your anxiety is to take control and be positive. If you feel negative and do nothing, your worry levels will rise and you will experience more stress. If you feel positive and are taking positive action, your worry levels will fall and you will feel less stressed.

Your frame of mind is the essential element in determining your levels of worry. Many parents spend a great deal of time worrying and very little time enjoying family life. If you are feeling negative, the feeling of worry can become all-consuming and is always in your mind. If you're negative, you give anxiety the opportunity to rear its ugly head as often as it wants.

Many parents find they spend huge amounts of time worrying about things they cannot possibly change. Many others spend hours worrying about what **might** happen rather than what is happening. For many mums and dads, worrying is their natural state. They're used to being permanently worried and this has just become a normal part of life for them. They're always worrying – it's just the level of worry that may vary from day to day.

There may be certain circumstances in your life that you cannot change, but you can change the way you respond to them. There may be people in your life that you worry about. You may not be able to change them or their situations, but you can change the way you deal with the worry. There may be many things you worry about that you can do something positive about, but because you spend so much time worrying you never get around to doing it. These are the fundamental problems for many parents: wasting time worrying about things they can do nothing about or wasting time worrying instead of doing something to reduce the anxiety they feel. Remember, if you think you can, you can. If you think you can't, you can't.

How has worrying about anything ever helped you in your life to date? You may invest a huge amount of time and energy in worrying, but what positive impact has that ever had? We need to channel that time and energy in a much more positive way.

If you could replace your feelings of anxiety with a positive feeling instead, what positive feeling would you choose? One of the mums I worked with found this exercise very helpful. Tamsin spent so much time worrying, she'd never thought about how she'd like to spend her time feeling. She said that in an ideal world she wanted to feel positive, in control and calm. What three feelings would you choose? Rank them in order from one to three.

1.

2.

> 3.

■ What makes this top feeling so powerful for you?
■ What makes it your number one choice?
■ Think about how you can increase this positive feeling in your life
from today. What one specific action can you take today that will
increase that feeling in your life?

I want you to focus on boosting that positive feeling in everything you
do. Live that feeling. Breathe that feeling. Show it in your face. Enjoy it
in your heart. Live it through your actions. It's your most powerful
weapon against worry. If you are channelling your energy in a positive
way, negative feelings will find it much harder to get a look in.

Action

Take a look at the worry list you completed yesterday and put a mark next
to all the issues that you tend to worry about rather than doing something
about. Take a close look and really focus. For each item on the list, ask yourself the following key question.

Is there something I can actually **do** about this that will reduce the worry
I feel now? It may be a big thing or a small thing, but if there is something
you can do, put a mark next to it.

Once you have done this take a look at all the items you've marked and
identify the top three worries that you want to start taking control of. We're
going to move forward a step at a time.

1. _____

2. _____

3. _____

DAY 3: TACKLE YOUR WORRY LIST – ONE DAY AT A TIME

By now, you will be beginning to notice a difference in yourself and the way you feel. You're facing today in a positive state of mind that will help you to take positive and effective actions. You have already come a long way in reducing your worry levels and today we are going to move forward again.

Take a look at the list of the top three worries that you identified yesterday and decide which top worry you want to focus on. Remember that you identified them as worries that have a big impact on your life but that **you** can take practical steps to do something about to reduce the level of worry **you** feel.

Focus on the negative impact that this has on your life at the moment. Close your eyes and imagine the positive feeling that you want to replace the worry with. Breathe deeply and let it fill your whole body. Imagine what your life will be like if you can reduce the power of this particular worry on a day-to-day basis. What will be the most significant positive effect of being able to do this?

It is important to focus on one worry at a time. If you think about everything all at once you are likely to feel overwhelmed and this will make it more difficult for you to move forwards. Break the journey down into small steps – and take it a step at a time.

On a scale of 1 to 10, how anxious do you feel about the top worry you have identified? A score of 1 indicates a low level of anxiety and a score of 9 or 10 indicates an extremely high level of anxiety. Circle the number below that reflects the way you feel.

1 2 3 4 5 6 7 8 9 10

Your goal for today is to reduce that score by just a half or a whole point. So, if you've given yourself a worry score of 8 out of 10, we're going to take action to bring that score down to 7.5 or 7. The key to reducing stress and boosting energy is to take one successful step at a time. If you know where you want to be and you're always moving in the right direction, you will arrive at your destination.

Katy identified her top three as:

- ■ Worries about breast cancer.
- ■ Worries about finding a nursery.
- ■ Worries about family finances.

They were all big worries that impacted on her life and increased the stress she felt. She decided that her fear about her mortality – and especially breast cancer – was the big one for her. It was a great decision to focus on this. She said that once she'd done something about this fear, she would feel much better able to deal with the other worries, such as finding a nursery and family finances. Always remember that you are the engine driving your family. Often it can be hard to deal with worries affecting the family if there is something specific about you that is worrying you but that you are not dealing with. Putting yourself first isn't selfish, it's often the most effective way to act.

Katy's worries about her mortality and, specifically, breast cancer were very typical of many of the mums I work with. Just like them, she was spending lots of time worrying about what might happen rather than enjoying her valuable time with her family.

To begin with, I asked Katy to focus specifically on what was worrying her about this issue and the negative impact it was having on her. That was the problem. Then I asked her to focus on the solution – what would that look like for her? What would she need to know or be doing that would replace those negative worries with positive feelings? What specifically would reduce her anxiety about this issue? I then asked her to complete the Worry Action Wheel, brainstorming seven ideas that she could think of that would help move her away from the worry and towards the solution. They needed to be practical actions that she could control, things that she could do herself to reduce her worries about breast cancer.

This is what her Worry Action Wheel looked like. As you'll see, it made her think about the big picture regarding her health and fitness.

Completing the wheel really helped to reduce the impact of Katy's anxieties because she had come up with a whole list of actions that she

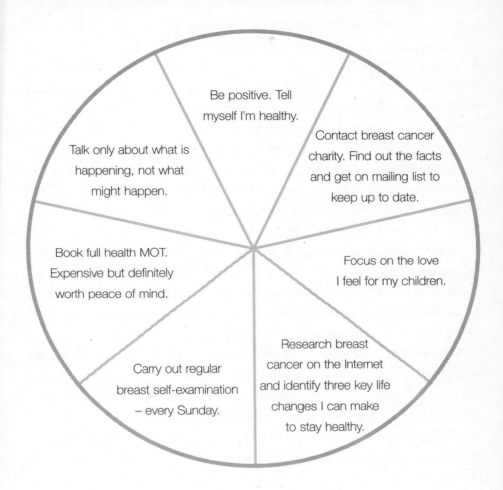

could actually take to reduce the worry in her life. She was taking positive steps forwards. Focusing on the strong positive feelings of love for her children and sending a positive message about her health to herself really helped to reduce Katy's stress levels. She said this exercise was a wake up call, making her realise just how much valuable time she was spending sending herself and other people very negative messages. The decision to contact the breast cancer charity was a key one. She was actually scared about lots of things to do with the illness that she knew very little about. By making the decision to contact the charity and find out more, it meant that she would be properly informed and know the facts. It meant she had a real idea of the chances of getting the disease and some excellent practical advice about useful lifestyle changes she could make.

Ram was desperate to stop smoking. When he was completing his Worry Action Wheel, he wanted to think of something so powerful that it would stop him reaching for a cigarette. It only took him a few minutes to come up with the answer. He closed his eyes and pictured his family at his funeral, gathered around his grave. All his children were there. He pictured their faces clearly and he could see they were sobbing. Every time he felt like a cigarette, he concentrated on that picture in his mind. It was extremely powerful. He hasn't smoked since. It is a shocking image that worked for him.

You will have your own ideas, ones that work for you. You are the expert on your own life.

Now complete your own Worry Action Wheel opposite. Firstly, focus on what makes your number one worry the big one for you and think hard about its impact on you. Secondly, focus on what the solution looks like and what you need to know or do that will help to reduce your negative feelings about this particular issue. Thirdly, brainstorm your worry action list. In each segment of the wheel, write down one practical action that you can take that will reduce the level of anxiety you feel about this issue. Remember, you have to be able to take an action to support each idea.

Action

Make sure you complete each segment of the wheel. You have now identified seven great actions that you know will enable you to reduce your stress levels where this particular issue is concerned.

Take a look at all the ideas you have put in your Worry Action Wheel. Focus on each one in turn and think clearly about how completing this action will help to reduce the power that the worry has over you. What impact will it have on you and your frame of mind that will help you to feel more positive and in control?

Now rank your ideas from one to seven. They are all ideas that will help

WORRY ACTION

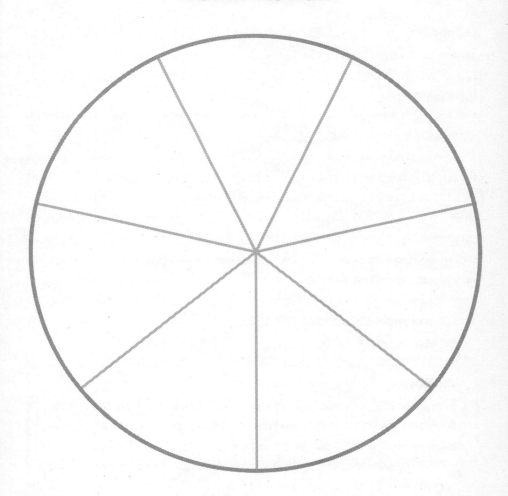

you to move forwards. Your number one idea will be the action that you would most like to do first.

1. _____

2. _____

3. _____

4. _____

5. _____

6. _____

7. _____

Put an action a day into your diary. This means that by this time next week, you will have made significant moves forwards in decreasing the power of the worry.

Remember, it is essential that you believe you can do this. The power of the worry in your life is increased by negative thinking and lack of control. You are beginning to take control, but this will only be effective if it is coupled with your self-belief that you can change things. You can, so do it.

DAY 4: WORKOUT WITH YOUR OWN PERSONAL TRAINER – YOUR CHILDREN

By the end of today, I want you to feel that you have taken a huge step forward in terms of feeling healthy and reducing the negative thoughts you have about your own health. I'm going to make it as easy as possible for you to do this. Relax. I'm not going to ask you to sign up to a year's membership of the local gym – but feel free to do this if you want to. My health MOT is easy and practical and you're going to really enjoy the benefits straight away.

If you are feeling healthy, motivated, dynamic and energetic, it is much easier to handle your worries effectively and successfully. If you are feeling unhealthy, tired and vulnerable, the smallest niggles can quickly become major worries and increase your stress levels.

So it's important you do everything possible to feel healthy instead of feeling unhealthy. Parents are notoriously bad at looking after themselves and extremely good at giving themselves a very hard time. We make it incredibly easy to convince ourselves that we're unhealthy. Just think about the messages you send yourself and other people. There are lots of things you may do on a daily basis that you think you shouldn't be doing because they're unhealthy, such as using the car, microwaving your children's meals, having a drink, watching TV and eating a biscuit. When was the last time you thought to yourself or said to someone, 'I'm not as healthy as I should be'?

When it comes to feeling healthy, quite the opposite is true. We set the bar really high for ourselves. Parents are the worst. We can make it incredibly difficult to convince ourselves that we're healthy. We seem to think that unless we're doing everything perfectly – power walking every morning, drinking litres of water, going to the gym three times a week, cutting out chocolate, walking everywhere, taking the children swimming, cutting out alcohol – we don't have the right to call ourselves healthy. When we don't achieve the ideal, we convince ourselves we're failing. When was the last time you thought to yourself or said to someone, 'I feel really fit and healthy'?

As you know, the key to the way you feel lies in your state of mind. If you are consistently thinking negative thoughts about your health, you will feel more unhealthy. So stop thinking and start doing.

As parents, we're in the fortunate position of having our very own personal trainers – our children! What do you think about being a mum or a dad and how it impacts on your health? You often hear parents commenting on the fact that they find having children exhausting (fantastic but fatiguing) and talking a lot about how tired they feel. Some of the parents I've coached have said that they feel they've become quite obsessive about how tired they are and how many hours of sleep they may or may not have had. Sleep deprivation is a form of torture and it's easy to understand why parents fall into the habit of talking about this.

But the more you talk about being tired, the worse you will feel, so don't do it. It will just make you feel more tired and more stressed. Do you ever say to other parents, 'Are you alright? You look tired.' You may say this because you want to show that you care, but how do you think it makes them feel? How would it make you feel if someone said that to you? The effect is likely to make you feel worse than you do already.

Let's re-frame this experience. Instead of thinking about all the different ways that children drain your energy, think about how they increase your vitality and zest for life. Your children are probably the best personal trainers you could have. They're around 24/7. They have loads of energy – lots of get up and go. They can keep you incredibly fit if you want them to. They provide your biggest motivation to stay healthy, a constant reminder of what makes it important to be fit and well. You want to be around for as long as possible for them.

Complete your Child Trainer Wheel opposite. I want you to fill it with seven activities that you currently do with your children that are good for your health. Think very carefully about what you do on a daily basis. There will probably be lots of things that you do already – but perhaps don't give a second thought to. You don't think about them because you are working so hard to give yourself a hard time and nurture that unhealthy inner parent! Your list is unique to you, think about everything possible that can go into it. It might include, for example, running up and down the stairs (toilet training for toddlers), carrying children/shopping to or from the car (weights), giving piggy backs, walking, pushing a swing in the park, laughing, swimming ... the list is endless.

Action

Commit today to telling yourself all the reasons you are healthy instead of all the reasons that you are not. Every time you look at your children, see your

CHILD TRAINER

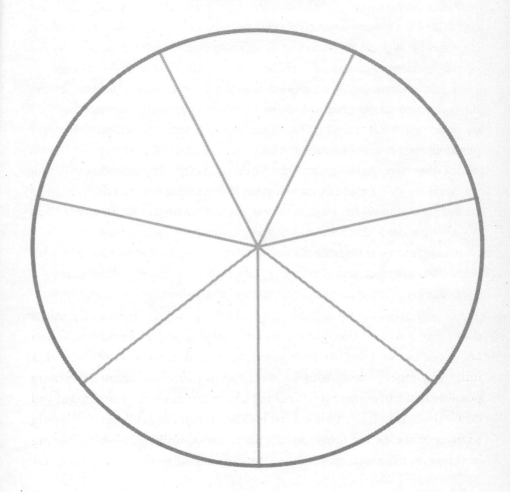

own personal trainers who love you unconditionally and want you to be around – happy and healthy – for as long as possible.

This week, **every time** that you do one of the actions on your Child Trainer Wheel, I want you to say out loud, 'I am healthy and climbing the stairs' ... 'I'm healthy and walking with my child' ... 'I'm healthy and lifting my child up' ... 'I'm healthy and laughing' ... 'I'm healthy and sharing an apple with my child' ...

Make a conscious effort to focus on everything you do with your children that is good for you. Don't let anything pass by without your verbal recognition.

Ensure that you avoid making negative comments over the next 24 hours, such as how tired you feel or how unhealthy you are. This may take practice but you can do it. Don't say anything negative to other parents about the way they look or feel, either.

Every time you do something positive, you put it in the health bank. You can carry this across into every aspect of life. Tell yourself you are feeling healthy when you drink a glass of water (it doesn't have to be litres) or eat an apple (it's a good first step towards the five fruit and vegetables you should have each day). Make it easy, not difficult, for yourself to feel healthy.

Make feeling healthy easy and fun. You'll be amazed at how much healthier you feel in just 24 hours – and you'll be transformed in seven days.

DAY 5: CHALLENGE YOUR CHILDREN'S NEGATIVE VIEW OF THE WORLD

Today I want you to focus on you and your children. As we've discovered this week, many parents live in a world of worry. Their children inhabit this world too. They have no choice.

Many parents are very careful about trying to protect their children from worries, but your children have great intuition, just like you. They know you well. They pick up messages from you in all sorts of ways – just as you do from them. They know when you're stressed. They know when you're happy.

So actually, by worrying about things for the right reason (you want the best for them) you may be impacting negatively on their world. Start to be aware of that today.

Your focus is on your children today. Focus on everything they say and do. Make a conscious effort to gauge whether their words and actions indicate that they're living in a world with worries and negative thoughts or whether they are positive and carefree.

When Cheryl, one of my clients carried out this exercise, she was surprised at how anxious her daughter Kelly seemed to be about a range of things. Cheryl hadn't really noticed before. She was sure her daughter was no different, it was just that Cheryl hadn't been tuned in to the way Kelly was acting and the language she was using. The worry list covered a whole range of things. Kelly worries about passing a dog, the dark nights drawing in, not being able to find a crayon, putting on shoes and taking the top off a yogurt pot.

Cheryl's experience is shared by many mums and dads. Your children may often be doing and saying things that you have become so used to that you hardly notice. You need to tune into them specifically. Just like many of us, children can waste a great deal of time worrying about what might happen rather than what is happening. Don't let them do it. Encourage them to spend their time focusing on what is happening or taking action to overcome their worries. You want this attitude to become a way of life for them. It will be a great foundation for adult life.

If your children say anything negative about themselves or the world today, challenge them and help them understand why this isn't the case. Help them to convert the problems that worry them into solutions that thrill them. Motivate them to live in a 'can do', not a 'can't do' world. It's so much more fun.

Take little Kelly's anxiety about passing a dog. I asked Cheryl what she could do when this happened again that would help convert Kelly's negative world view into a positive one. Cheryl decided that instead of just reassuring Kelly that the dog wouldn't bite, she would make a point of explaining that Kelly's fears were unfounded and talk in a very positive way about the dog. They'd ask the owner to talk about the dog too and what they love about it.

Instead of simply reassuring Kelly that the dark evenings shouldn't scare her because she was with her mum, Cheryl decided to embark on a campaign to make the darkness as exciting as possible. Every time they were out in the dark, or they looked at the dark from inside the home, Cheryl made the experience an adventure ... for both of them. In the end, rather than stay as far away as possible from the dark, Kelly wanted to engage with it. Cheryl had been very successful in converting a negative into a positive.

Of course, like every parent, Cheryl wants Kelly to grow up being wise about the possible risks posed by unfriendly dogs or the dark, but she wants her daughter to be wise from a positive starting point based on fact – not a negative one based on fiction. Cheryl doesn't want Kelly to grow up being negative and scared and letting her imagination run riot so that she's constantly expecting the worst. She wants Kelly to grow up being positive and expecting the best, making wise decisions based on fact. Cheryl has taken the first steps.

Action

What are your child's three top worries? Rank them from one to three. Focus on their top worry.

- How does it manifest itself?
- What do they say or do to indicate they are anxious?
- What action can you take to help?
- What specific feeling would you like to replace the feelings of anxiety that your children may demonstrate?
- What is the single biggest reason for choosing it?
- How will it benefit your children if you can boost this feeling in their day-to-day lives?
- When you are with your children today, focus on the positive feeling you have chosen. How can you boost that feeling in their lives?

Your children are never too young to start talking about positive feelings. Focus on something specific to do with them that will increase this feeling in them. Be as creative as you can. It may be to talk or dance or sing or play, to read a story, act a story, create a picture or just tickle or cuddle them. You are the expert in your own situation so you choose, but focus specifically on feeling positive, and a practical way that you can bring this into your life and the lives of your children. If you create a picture, put it somewhere clearly visible in your home so that you and they will see it as often as possible and talk about it.

DAY 6:
FOCUS AND HAVE FUN!

As I mentioned at the beginning of this week, the real problem with worrying is that it stops you enjoying family life. You are so concerned about what might happen, or about not being in control, that the negative you takes hold and it is difficult to get back in touch with all the positive feelings you have about being a mum or dad.

One of the most effective ways to be more positive is to enjoy your children – and I mean really enjoy them.

Mums and dads often do things with their children that could be really enjoyable but – for many reasons – are not. This may be because the parents don't have their minds on what they are doing. They are thinking and worrying about so many other things.

Today is going to be different. You need to experience this to know how powerful this feeling can be. The feeling of really enjoying your children has the potential to reduce the power of worry significantly – but you have to commit to doing this properly.

I want you to get in touch with the fun, childlike qualities that you possess. You may have spent so much time being worried about adult things that you have forgotten what this feels like but it is really important for you and your children that you can have fun. It doesn't matter how old you are. This is not only something you can enjoy, it also means you're likely to live longer.

In the Fun Wheel opposite, write down seven fun things that you can do by yourself or with your children. What can you do that will give you a real opportunity to get back in touch with the child in you, to be adventurous, to be carefree, to giggle and to laugh? They can be very simple things – so simple that often you just don't think about doing them. What do you really want to put on your list? This is your chance to be a child for a while and put adult worries behind you. They need to be things that you can do over the next week. You are in control of your own fun, so boost it. You are not dependent on anyone else, so go for it.

One of my clients, Jonathan, had an extremely heavy workload and so, although he loved spending time with his children, he never seemed to be relaxed with them. He identified the problem. When he was with his children he was usually also thinking about issues he had to sort out at work. He said that whatever he was doing with the children always seemed to get pushed into second place because his mind was pre-occupied with work worries. Jonathan completed his Fun Wheel and for one weekend committed to focusing only on having fun with his children. He said that this made him realise just how much time and energy he invested in work activities and how little in family activities – he tended to just let those happen, by chance. His job was extremely well paid, so the children didn't want for much in a material sense. But Jonathan knew that he wasn't giving his children what they really wanted, and that was his time and attention.

Jonathan's top fun idea was to put up a tent in the back garden and sleep there overnight with his two boys. The family had never camped before but his little boys were desperate to try it because they had friends who went camping regularly. Jonathan borrowed some camping gear. He cooked them all dinner on a stove. He sat in the darkness of the tent and told the children a wonderful story about a dinosaur that worked on the moon. The dinosaur's job was to teach the new stars how to shine brightly, and he did this by tickling them. Everyone had lots of tickles and laughs. It was a very special evening and then Dad and the children snuggled together for the night.

When Jonathan was reporting back to me, he was amazed by the difference it had made in the way he felt about himself and life. He'd

FUN

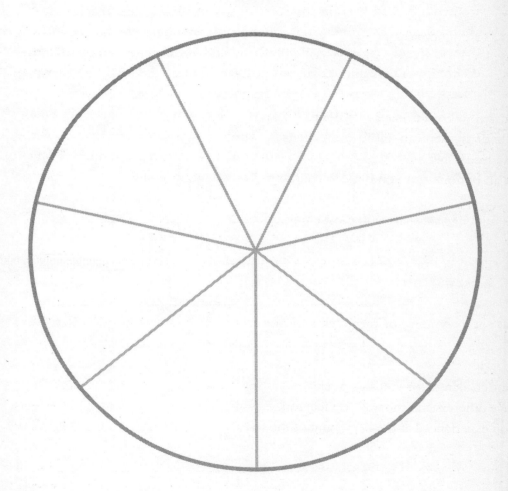

managed to leave his load of worries at the office for the weekend and just enjoy being a dad. He said that he began to feel like the real Jonathan again – the one he'd lost touch with – and it was so wonderful to see the children sharing his fun. The dinosaur story is still the family favourite! When Jonathan went into work on Monday morning, there was a real bounce in his step. When his colleagues asked him about his weekend, he had been in the habit of saying, 'It was fine thanks. How about you?' This Monday was different. 'It was fantastic,' he said. 'The best weekend I've ever had.' Both he and his colleagues noticed the difference in his outlook. He was positive and 'can do' – and a lot more effective in his two roles: as managing director and Dad.

So, now it is your turn. Fill in your Fun Wheel and enjoy the time you spend doing it.

Now rank your Fun Wheel from one to seven with the number one being the action that you feel most excited about doing.

1. _____

2. _____

3. _____

4. _____

5. _____

6. _____

7. _____

Action

Take out your diary and put your fun ideas in it – one fun idea per day. It may take a little more planning but put something down for every day this week.

Complete your first fun activity today. Before you begin, make sure that you are focusing only on the positive. Banish all negative thoughts from your mind, even if it is only for the next 10 minutes. If you can do this, you will feel more positive at the end of those 10 minutes and you will have reduced the impact that your worries have on you.

DAY 7:
ANXIETY UPDATE

You have now reached day seven of your action plan. By completing each of the daily exercises you will have come a long way in establishing a strategy that will help you to reduce your anxiety levels. You've learned lots of different techniques and should be spending more time living and less time worrying.

You know already that the process of worrying does not reduce the anxiety you feel about any issue. The key to reducing your anxiety is to invest time in positive action to address the issues that concern you, rather than wasting time on negative thoughts. The more you worry, the more worried you will feel. The more you enjoy life, the more enjoyment you will get out of life. By now, you will be beginning to reap the benefits of everything positive you have done this week.

You have:

- Started to take control by conducting an effective anxiety audit.
- Committed to channelling your energy in a positive, not a negative way.
- Created an action plan to tackle your worry list – one worry at a time.
- Started working out with your own personal trainers – your children.
- Challenged any negative view of the world that your children may have.
- Spent time having fun instead of wasting time worrying.

At the beginning of the week, I asked you to rate your anxiety levels on a scale of 1 to 10. Take a look back at the score you gave yourself. A score of 1 indicated low levels of anxiety and a score of 10 indicated high levels of worry.

■ What Anxiety Score did you have before? _____

■ How do you feel now that you have completed your 7-day action plan?

■ What levels of anxiety do you feel now? Circle the number that applies.

1   2   3   4   5   6   7   8   9   10

Well done. Taking the decision to face your worries and do something about them is a really brave step. It can be so much easier to do nothing and hope that they go away. Of course, they never do.

You will be feeling more positive and more in control. You will feel less stressed and more energetic. Think back over the past seven days and focus on just how far you have come. Now look forward to the next seven days and commit to staying in touch with all that you enjoy about being a mum or dad.

Think about how you felt at the beginning of the week when you were keeping your worry diary, and how you feel today.

■ What has been the biggest challenge for you this week?

■ What is the biggest positive difference in the way you feel today compared with the feelings you experienced on day one?

■ What positive impact has this had on your relationship with yourself and with your children?

Read your Parent Achievement Log (see page 291) for this week and recognise all that you have achieved. Take your time and enjoy the feeling of achievement. Focus on the difference you are making to yourself and to your family by thinking and acting positively and taking control.

Now rank your achievements from one to seven with number one being the achievement that has had the biggest impact on you and your family this week.

1. _____

2. _____

3. _____

4. _____

5. _____

6. _____

7. _____

■ What makes this your biggest achievement of the week?
■ What impact has it had on you?
■ What impact has it had on your relationship with your children?
■ How does that feel?

Action

Today, I want you to spend time writing a letter to your children. Tell them what you love most about them. If today were the very last time you were ever going to see them, what would you say to them about the amazing difference they have made to your life?

■ What do they say that you'll always remember?
■ What little things make them the wonderful people they are today?

Be as specific as you can in each sentence. This is a letter they will treasure forever. Make some time to do this when you have peace and quiet.

Write about the huge difference they have made to you and how being a mum or dad has changed your life forever and brought all sorts of positive feelings that you would never have experienced without children.

■ How has being a mum or dad really helped you to grow as a person?

Make sure your letter includes all the things that you feel positive about, in terms of yourself, your children and your relationship with them.

■ What is special about the bond you have with your children – the special bond that no-one can ever take away?

This is a very positive letter. Think of everything you've got to feel positive about in your life and set it down in black and white. Writing this will help you to focus on the positive and not the negative.

Tonight, before you go to bed, I want you to give your children a cuddle and read this letter out loud. Put the letter by your bed so that it is the last thing you read every night this week. If you do this, you will go to sleep focusing on everything you have to be positive about, rather than on your negative thoughts. Whenever you feel niggling or overwhelming worries, I want you to focus what is written in this letter. Don't give way to the power of negative thoughts.

chapter eight
confident parents
create children 'who can'

The other day, I saw a little boy in the local park kicking a ball at a goal made up of his mother's shoes. He kicked the ball from a make-believe penalty spot into the goal again .... and again ... and again. Once he'd kicked it, he'd run to collect the ball and start again. Most of his shots were on target but occasionally he kicked wide. He was totally focused on the task in hand. When he missed, he was clearly disappointed with his performance – kicking the ground 'Premier League-style' – but he never gave up. He just tried and tried and tried again.

His mum on the other hand, told him not to worry when he failed to score a goal. 'You can't score every time, Zachary,' she called. 'It doesn't matter.'

But it did matter to him. 'I can,' Zachary called back, 'I can score every time.'

Well, with focus and self-belief like this, Zachary may well have what it takes to make the England team. I'm sure they'd certainly appreciate a young talent determined to score and not likely to throw a tantrum on the field. But, observing this scene, what was so special, was the powerful feeling of confidence that Zachary had in himself and his abilities – and the way his mum was dealing with it.

His mum was trying to be helpful so that he wouldn't be disappointed on the occasions that he failed to score. For all the best reasons, she was lowering his aspirations. Zachary was having none of that. He wanted to be the best and do the best and he believed in himself.

Confidence is absolutely fundamental in all that you do. It reduces your stress, increases your energy and helps you to achieve your goals. Confidence will also help you to create children 'who can' instead of children 'who can't'. If you're one of the many parents whose confidence could do with a turbo-boost, here's a 7-day action plan for you. Make small changes every day and you'll notice a big difference by the end of the week. We're going to explore the area of confidence and get to grips with positive strategies to boost your confidence – and your children's.

This is what makes confidence such a vital quality. If you think you can, you will be able to. If you think you can't, you won't be able to. If your children think they can, they can. If they think they can't, they can't. With confidence, all things are possible. Without it, nothing is possible.

The majority of parents I work with say that their confidence has taken a knock as a result of having a child. Now, this isn't at all surprising. Being responsible for yourself is one thing but suddenly becoming responsible for a little person who is totally dependent on you is quite another. Children don't come with a handy instruction booklet. Everything's new, so lack of confidence is very common in parenting. You are committed to making the best decisions and doing the best job possible, but it's a 24-hour challenge so it's only natural to feel vulnerable. In fact, this is a positive quality. It means you are constantly assessing and developing your parenting role.

CONFIDENCE BOOSTING

The mums who go out to work feel particularly vulnerable to a lack of confidence. A survey by the national charity Parentalk reveals that two out of three working mothers lose confidence after having a baby. They even believed that colleagues thought they were less able to do their jobs once they became mothers. The mums didn't think this because work colleagues had made comments to that effect. It was entirely to do with the way that working mothers believed their colleagues perceived them.

Their reduced confidence affected their view of themselves and the way they thought others regarded them. Lack of confidence is a natural feeling, especially with mums who rarely focus on the things they do well but are brilliant at telling people what they don't or can't do.

But if you can boost your confidence, you'll help build your children's confidence. Confidence is a great gift to your children and the first step is to build confidence in yourself.

I want you to begin by focusing on the word 'confidence' and think very carefully about what it means to you. Think of a time when you have felt really confident in your life. It can be about anything at all. You choose. Focus on the positive way it made you feel. What was the very best thing about feeling that confident?

What is the worst thing about lacking confidence? Think of one key thing that lack of confidence has stopped you from doing in your life.

Think about how confident you feel in yourself today. We will be focusing on your confidence as a parent a little later, but for now, just concentrate on the whole you. The reason for this is that your confidence as a person will have a direct impact on your confidence as a parent, so it is important to look at the bigger life picture first.

On a scale of 1 to 10, how confident do you feel? A score of 1 indicates low levels of confidence. A score of 10 indicates high confidence levels. Mark your confidence score below:

$$1 \quad 2 \quad 3 \quad 4 \quad 5 \quad 6 \quad 7 \quad 8 \quad 9 \quad 10$$

Who has the biggest influence over how confident you feel in yourself? Is it you? Or is your confidence influenced by what others say or think about you? A robust confidence is built from within. You have the ability to believe in yourself and that is the strongest confidence you can have. If you spend your life being dependent on what other people say or think about you – this will be a fragile confidence. It is outside your control. The same applies to your children's confidence in themselves.

The greatest obstacle to a more confident you is – you. The more time you spend sending out the powerful negative message that you're not confident, the less confident you will feel. It's a vicious circle and it's important to act today to break it.

Action

Smile more often. This is so simple and yet extremely effective. Sometimes we're so busy dealing with the challenges of life that we forget all the things we have to be positive about. There will be lots. Sometimes we just have to remind ourselves what they are.

There's so much for you to smile about, especially when you think about your children. They love you unconditionally. Smiling will not only make you feel much more positive and confident, it will also build their confidence and they'll feel valued. They'll grow up feeling secure with the message that adulthood is something to look forward to – not dread.

Give your children a big cuddle. If you focus on all the reasons you have **to feel confident** about being a parent, the more confident you will become. There's no such thing as a perfect parent, but you know you are doing your best. Be proud of that.

- What else have you achieved?
- What qualities make you a good mum or dad?

Say the answers to these questions out loud.

It's really important that we acknowledge our achievements as parents. Each day I want you to make a note of your biggest achievement (see Parent Achievement Log, page 291). It may be something you achieve when you're carrying out your daily coaching action. Or it may be something that just happens in the course of the day and you think to yourself, 'Yes! That was great!' You decide what is significant for you.

DAY 2: TURBO-BOOST YOUR CONFIDENCE

Today, I want you to focus on ways of boosting your confidence in all areas of your life.

People often talk about confidence as though it is a quality you either have or you don't have. It is talked about as an intangible concept that is outside your control. If you have confidence, you are fortunate. If you don't have confidence, you are unfortunate.

I believe that you can take control and boost your own confidence. Your confidence – or lack of it – is within your control and this means that you have the ability to boost it.

Make a list of your three biggest achievements in life so far.

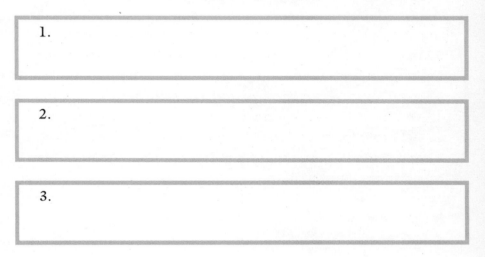

1.

2.

3.

■ When you look at them, how do you feel?
■ What makes these your most significant achievements?
■ What impact did they have on your confidence?

I believe that you can boost your confidence by setting yourself tangible goals that you can achieve. Break down big targets into small achievable steps. The key is that they all be goals that are within your control.

I asked one of my mothers, Gill, to complete the Confidence Wheel below. She'd come to me saying she rarely felt confident, so there was lots of room for improvement. She had separated from her partner a year earlier and was struggling to come to terms with the break up and bringing up the children on her own.

I asked Gill to complete her personal Confidence Wheel, identifying seven things that she could do that would make her feel more confident. I asked her to think big – and small. This is what her Confidence Wheel looked like:

I asked Gill to identify her priority action. What was the one thing that would have the biggest positive impact on her confidence. For Gill, it was being able to say 'no' because she kept agreeing to things that she didn't want to do. She wanted friends and family to like her, so she was saying 'yes' when she wanted to say 'no'. As a result, she was spreading herself too thin, trying to do too much and was permanently stressed. She was feeling particularly anxious because she felt intimidated by some of the mothers at her son's playgroup who kept press-ganging her into activities that she didn't want to do.

Gill was stressed and devoid of energy because many aspects of her life were outside her control. She was handing control over to other people and so she was feeling very negative.

For the next week she committed to saying 'no' whenever she was asked to do something that she really didn't want to do. She practised saying 'no' in a very positive way that wasn't at all defensive. She rehearsed what she was going to say in front of the mirror until she felt well prepared and had the confidence to say 'no'.

Gill called me the first time she achieved her 'no'. She said she felt wonderful and in control for the first time in months. The other mum had been really understanding.

Gill now had the time to do what she wanted to do, instead of what other people wanted her to do. A big result. She also said that taking a minute to put on some lipstick each day had really boosted her confidence, too.

She was moving forwards, a step at a time.

Action

Complete your own Confidence Wheel overleaf. In each segment, write down something that you can do that will boost your confidence this week. Remember, the key is to ensure that everything you put in your wheel is within your control. That is the only way that you can ensure that you will achieve it.

Once the wheel is completed, you will have seven positive actions that you can take this week. Choose one goal that you can achieve in the next 24 hours. Work out exactly when you will do it and book it into your diary. Set yourself a positive goal that you can achieve. It may be frightening, but do it anyway!

Now put the remaining six actions into your diary on a specific day and at a specific time, if possible. Take a small step every day and by the end of this week, you will feel that your confidence has been boosted. If neccessary, enlist the help of a friend and support each other.

CONFIDENCE

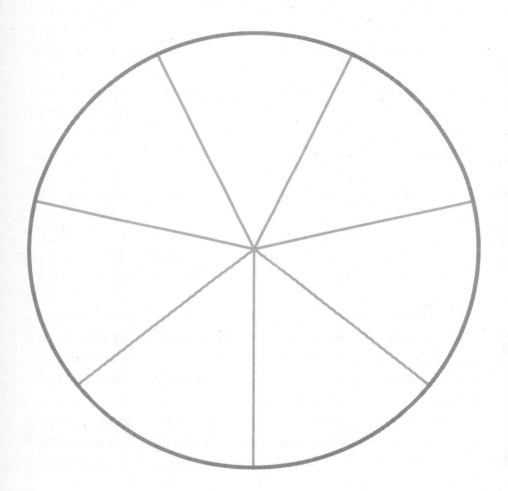

DAY 3:
STOP CONFIDENCE THIEVES

The next step is to start talking yourself up instead of down. Parents are great at undermining their own confidence. They'll list everything they haven't done, or should have done or could have done better, quicker than you can say 'Thomas The Tank Engine'. This sends a powerful negative message to yourself and to everyone around you. It drains your confidence. The more you send out this message, the less confident you feel.

Parents will rarely acknowledge everything they achieve on a daily basis. Today, you're going to change all that. Say only positive things about yourself today. Instead of saying you're tired because your little one isn't sleeping, talk about what you love about being a mum or dad. Instead of saying that juggling work and family is stressful, focus on what you enjoy most about combining motherhood with a career.

Remember that the key to building confidence is you and what you believe about yourself. By talking yourself up you are starting the powerful process of sending positive messages to yourself and everyone around you. This will help you boost your own confidence.

The next stage is to stop other people undermining your confidence. Many of us are affected by what our friends, family and colleagues say – we're only human, after all. If our confidence is totally dependent on other people telling us what a good job we're doing of a being a parent, it won't be a strong confidence.

You may have friends, family or colleagues who are having a bad day or who are predisposed to being negative. Confidence is too important a commodity to leave to them to provide. Commit to keeping your confidence within your control and don't hand it over to others.

I think that confidence feeds your life. It can be a powerful tool that will give you the frame of mind that makes anything possible. If your life is full of confidence, you will be able to propel yourself forward and boost your confidence at every stage. The best way to boost your confidence is to take control of it.

But, just as we have the power to boost our own confidence, we also have the power to drain it. And just as we give other people the power to boost our confidence, we can also give them the power to drain it.

Let's begin with you. Think about the beliefs that you hold about yourself that limit what you do. What are your three most limiting beliefs.

    1. I am ...

    2. I am ...

    3. I am ...

■ What impact have they had on your confidence and life to date?
■ What have they stopped you from doing?

One of my clients, Jenny, is the mother of three children under five. She does an amazing job bringing up her three wonderful children but she came to me because she was having a confidence crisis. She's returned to her job as a project manager with a multi-national company but said she'd lost confidence in her ability to do the work and this was having an impact on her confidence as a mum at home.

I asked Jenny to complete the Confidence Thieves Wheel and to write in it all the people that she came into contact with who she felt sometimes undermined her confidence in some way.

This is what it looked like:

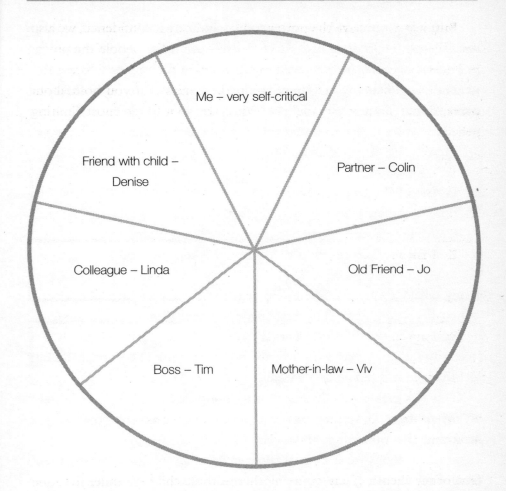

Jenny said that she felt guilty about putting these names down because they were all great people sometimes. It was just that occasionally, they would say something that undermined her confidence. Sometimes just the way they looked at her, without saying anything undermined her confidence. Because the comments or looks came from people whose opinion she valued, they had a powerful impact.

Jenny was wasting time imagining what people were thinking about her and letting this undermine her confidence instead of spending time taking positive steps to boost her own confidence.

I asked Jenny to think about specific comments that these people made that undermined her confidence and to list the three that had the most powerful negative impact.

Jenny found this to be a very interesting exercise. She identified three specific comments that had affected her confidence. These comments had taken on a life of their own in her mind and combined to create a general overwhelming feeling of lacking confidence. Her overwhelming perception of herself was that she was failing as a mother, a wife and a colleague and she believed that this was how her circle viewed her too.

Here is the list she came up with:

1. Partner: 'The children always seem to come first, we never have any time together.'
2. Colleague: 'You look tired – another sleepless night?'
3. Best friend: 'You shouldn't let those children rule you.'

Jenny talked about why she found that these three in particular undermined her confidence. The first made her feel that she was failing to deliver in her relationship. The second made her feel that she was a 'second-rate employee' who was not up to her job. The third made her feel that she was failing as a parent.

This was the way she had chosen to interpret what these people were saying to her. To Jenny they were negative comments that had a profound effect on her confidence.

I asked Jenny to think of alternative ways of interpreting these comments. If each of these people had meant something positive and not negative, what would they be trying to say to her? I was asking her to re-frame the comments that had been made to her and think about them in a different way.

She decided that each of them could be making the comment because they cared about her. These people wanted her to look after herself, or spend more time with them, because they valued her company as a partner, colleague or friend. I asked her to re-frame any negative comments she heard over the coming seven days into positive comments. It was up to her to decide whether these people would have an influence on her confidence.

Now take the time to complete your own Confidence Thieves Wheel.

In each segment of the circle, write the name of somebody who currently drains your confidence in some way. Underneath the circle,

CONFIDENCE THIEVES

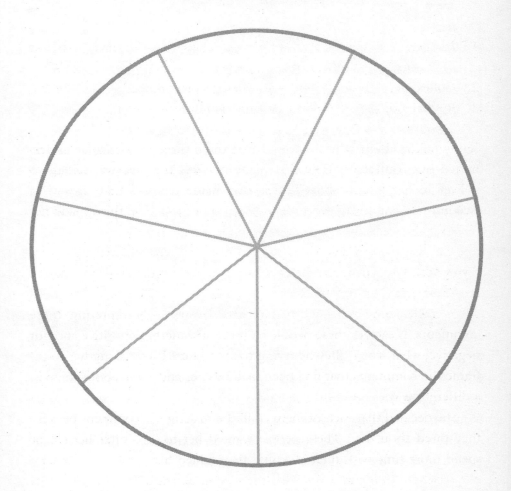

make a note of one thing they say that undermines your confidence. What is the comment that has had the biggest negative impact on you?

Now re-frame that comment in a positive way. If they were not intending it to be negative, how may they be expecting you to interpret what they are saying?

Action

Whenever somebody says something to you today that you feel undermines your confidence, re-frame it. Remember, the way you respond to anything others say is up to you. It can either boost your confidence or undermine it. Instead of convincing yourself that those closest to you doubt your ability, imagine they're actually amazed at how much you achieve.

This exercise will also make you more aware of the power of your own words. Today use only positive language with everyone you come in contact with. If you use positive language they are likely to use positive language back to you. If you use negative language, they are likely to use negative language back to you. Be an excellent role model for your children.

DAY 4:
BE A CONFIDENT PARENT

So far this week we have focused on boosting your confidence by setting confidence goals and removing confidence thieves. Today, I want you to focus on what will build your confidence as a parent.

On a scale of 1 to 10, how confident do you feel as a parent? Circle the number below that you think applies to you.

1   2   3   4   5   6   7   8   9   10

Imagine how you would feel if you felt 10 out of 10. How different would that feel from how you feel today?

I was coaching a mum, Megan. She has a son, Gus, who is nearly four and autistic, and Tilly, who is two. I asked Megan to complete the Parent

Confidence Wheel with a list of seven things she could do to boost her confidence as a parent.

Here is her Parent Confidence Wheel:

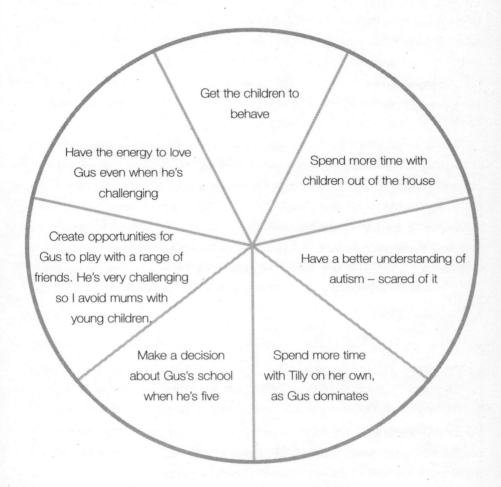

Get the children to behave

Have the energy to love Gus even when he's challenging

Spend more time with children out of the house

Create opportunities for Gus to play with a range of friends. He's very challenging so I avoid mums with young children.

Have a better understanding of autism – scared of it

Make a decision about Gus's school when he's five

Spend more time with Tilly on her own, as Gus dominates

I asked Megan to think again about 'getting the children to behave'. In order to boost her confidence, her goals need to be within her control. I asked her what she could do herself that might make a difference to the children's behaviour. What would be a small step that she could take. She identified that her priority would be to stop shouting at the children so much and to try to find alternative ways to deal with their challenging behaviour.

I asked Megan to rank these parent confidence boosters from one to seven with number one being the action that would have the biggest positive impact on her confidence as a parent.

It was a tough decision. All the things on her list had the potential to make a huge impact on her life. She opted for creating opportunities for Gus to play with a range of friends. His behaviour was often so challenging that she consciously avoided spending time with mums with other young children because she was worried they would find him so stressful. She thought that if she did this, it would build her confidence in the way she handled the children.

I asked her which single thing she could do over the coming week to make this happen. She decided she would like to contact the two mums she liked most who had children of similar ages and arrange play dates for the coming week. She hadn't done this for months. Making this happen had a truly liberating effect on Megan. She found it helpful to talk to the other mums about her challenges as a parent and they were incredibly supportive. Gus and Tilly responded well to their new friends and Megan felt generally calmer and less stressed. As a result she shouted at the children less.

Action

Complete the Parent Confidence Wheel opposite. Make a list of seven things that you can do that will boost your confidence as a parent. Remember, the key is that everything on your list must be within your control – not your children's!

Once you have completed the wheel, you will have seven actions that you can take that will boost your confidence and reduce your stress levels.

Put one action a day into your diary over the coming week and take the first step in achieving each one of them.

■　How will you feel when you have achieved each one?
■　What difference will it make to your confidence as a parent?

Remember, building confidence is about taking small steps to achieve goals

PARENT CONFIDENCE

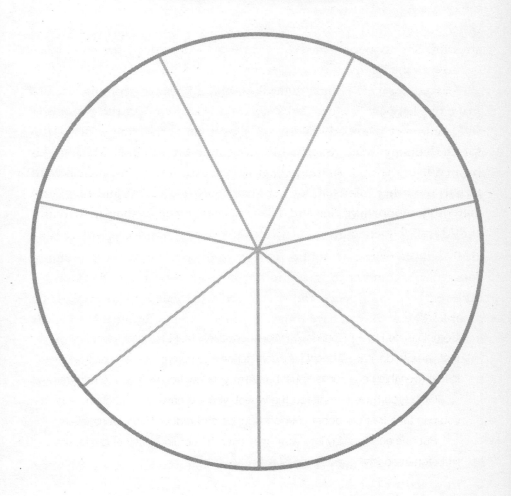

that are within your control. Take a step at a time and you'll discover just how quickly you can transform yourself and your family life.

Make sure that your Parent Achievement Log (see page 291) is up to date by completing it every day. This is a valuable record of your journey as a parent. Whenever you're in need of a quick confidence fix, look through it to remind yourself just how much you have achieved so far.

DAY 5: CREATE CHILDREN 'WHO CAN'

Today, I want you to focus on your children. When parents talk to me about what they want for their children, they usually say they want them to be happy and confident and believe in themselves. What wonderful gifts to give our children.

By taking the time to read this chapter, you have already made a valuable decision. You have found time in your busy day because building your child's confidence is a priority for you. So far this week we've explored your confidence and discovered what can help to boost it or drain it. The work you have done on yourself will be invaluable today as it means you have a good foundation on which to build a positive strategy to create confidence in your children.

On a scale of 1 to 10, how confident would you say your children are? Circle the number below that applies.

1   2   3   4   5   6   7   8   9   10

- In which area of life would you say your children are most confident?
- In which area of life would you say your children are least confident?
- Building confidence in which area of your children's life would have the biggest positive impact on them?

In the Child Confidence Wheel opposite, write down seven things that you can help your children to achieve that will boost their confidence.

CHILD CONFIDENCE

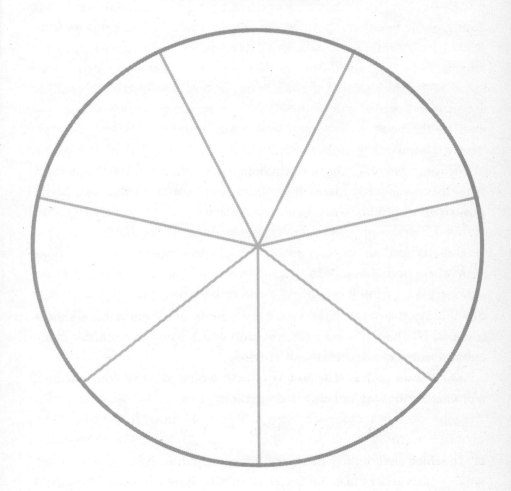

Remember, confidence can be built by setting practical goals that your children are committed to achieving – small steps to a big difference.

Once you have completed the wheel, you will have seven great ways to boost your children's confidence over the coming week. Choose one idea to focus on each day this week and put them in your diary to make sure that they happen.

Janice, one of the mums I was coaching, had a son, Tony, who loved going to the swimming pool but would never ask the lifeguards for armbands he could use. Normally, a confident child, approaching the lifeguards became a real issue for him and spoilt their enjoyment at the pool. Janice decided that she would like to help him work on this as her priority and turned the whole experience into a game. On the second visit to the pool, he managed it and was absolutely thrilled. Now he won't leave the lifeguards alone.

Siobhan wanted help to boost her son Noah's confidence. She came up with an idea that had radical results within days. Siobhan's a lovely conscientious mum wanting to encourage Noah in everything. She decided to focus on letting him do more of the things that he was good at and enjoyed, rather than trying to make him better at the things he wasn't so good at and didn't enjoy. It was a great idea – and we adults can learn a lot from it. We often spend more time trying to get better at the things we struggle with, rather than doing more of the things we're great at. Noah's confidence grew in leaps and bounds, making him much more positive about everything he tried.

Ossie was a dad who had been the main carer for his daughter, Veronica. Ossie and Veronica had a great relationship but he was worried that she wouldn't mix with other children. He identified the priority problem as those times when she was invited to children's birthday parties. She would cling to him and kick up a fuss. She refused to mix with other children if it meant leaving him. Party time had become a nightmare. Ossie said he believed that it would really boost her confidence if she felt able to do this.

Ossie brainstormed lots of different ways to achieve this: making regular play dates with other children; going to the soft play area where most of the parties took place so that she was familiar with it; getting

her mum to take her instead. But the key was for him to be more socia-
ble. He realised that his daughter was probably taking her lead from
him. He didn't feel confident in the company of other parents –
especially as he was often the only dad. In social situations, he would
isolate himself – keeping to himself at parties and also on a daily basis
when he took Veronica to the nursery. He committed to making a
real effort to mix with the other parents so that his daughter would
follow suit. On day one it was quite an ordeal at the doors of the nursery, but he went ahead and did it. He plunged into conversation with
a mum he hadn't spoken to before. The results were great, for both
Ossie and Veronica.

Now I want you to focus on other ways to boost your children's
confidence by asking great questions. Think for a moment or two about
what questions you can ask your children that will help to boost their
confidence. What are the top three that you have come up with?

1.

2.

3.

Wherever possible use 'open' not 'closed' questions. A 'closed' question
allows a child to give simple 'yes' or 'no' answers. An 'open' question will
encourage your children to talk and describe.

Throughout this chapter I have been reminding you that robust
confidence comes from within. This means that in order to give your
children the best possible start in life, you want to start building that
confidence from within as early as possible.

Many parents are good at praising their children when they do something well or behave well. This is helpful and certainly plays an important role in reinforcing good behaviour. But your praise is only part of the story. In order to establish excellent self-confidence, your children must have confidence in themselves and not just be dependent on what other people are saying to them. So, how can you help them to achieve this?

Step 1: Set a goal (or let them set their own goal) that is specific and can be measured so that you both know when it has been achieved.

Step 2: Help them to brainstorm as many ways as possible to achieve it. Be prepared to be surprised by their creativity.

Step 3: Talk with them as they achieve every stage in the process and ask them how they feel when they are doing it. It is important that from a very early age they learn to articulate their success, both to themselves and to other people.

Step 4: Develop a reward system that works for them. You can use praise, stickers or mark a chart, or let them draw stars or smiley faces or use ticks to indicate their success on their chart. This is part of the process of positive reinforcement.

Ask your children how they feel about what they are doing at every stage of the process. We aren't human doings – we are human beings. Talking about their positive feelings as they work towards achieving their goals will help to boost their confidence from the inside while you are boosting it from the outside. The earlier they start talking about their feelings the better. Help them to express everything they do and experience in a positive way. They say that the early years are a dress rehearsal for the teenage years. I believe that if you can get your little ones to be open about their feelings at an early stage, you are setting an excellent foundation for the years to come. Talk to them about their feelings now and they will talk to you about them in the future.

Many people lack confidence because they are dependent on other people praising them and telling them what a good job they are doing. By asking some simple questions, you are developing a positive plan to enable your children's confidence to grow from within.

Some of the parents I work with ask me what they can do to ensure that by focusing on ways of boosting children's confidence they don't end up pushing their children too hard and asking too much of them. The answer is simple. Listen to your heart. You are an intuitive mum or dad. Parents have a fantastic gut instinct about themselves, their parenting and their children. If you listen to yourself, you will know what is motivating you and you recognise when 'boosting confidence' becomes 'pushing children too hard'.

Action

Today I want you to focus on your children's confidence thieves – just as you did your own. Think really hard about the things that you say and the way that you say them that may have a negative impact on your children's confidence.

Think hard today about everything you say to your children and make sure it is confidence boosting, not confidence draining. Exploit every opportunity to let your children talk positively about themselves and their achievements.

DAY 6:
FAILING ISN'T AN OPTION

One of the best ways that you can help to boost your confidence – and your children's confidence – is get to grips with the concepts of 'success' and 'failure'.

Many people define their lives by their successes and their failures. Often it will be their failures that have the biggest negative impact on the way they feel about themselves and the way they believe other people feel about them.

Happy people are likely to be more successful because they are fundamentally happy in themselves. They are not driven by material or financial gain. This predisposes them to success. People who define success in terms of material or financial rewards only are less likely to be happy.

It is important for you as parents and for your children that you make success and failure work for you.

From today, I'd like you to eradicate the word 'fail' from your vocabulary. Everything that you do from now on in is a learning experience that actually helps you to grow and develop. You can either look at failures as negative experiences and be brought down by them or you can use them to move forward.

If I asked you to look back over your life and list one thing you feel you 'failed' at, what would you say?

I asked Bev, a client of mine, to do this and she was quite clear that her biggest failure was her marriage. She had divorced her husband and now felt guilty about being a lone parent.

I asked her to think about this in detail and to tell me three positive things that had come out of that apparent 'failure' of a marriage. If instead of seeing this as failing, she regarded it as a learning experience, what positives would she say came out of this?

At first Bev was silent. She said she couldn't think of anything that was positive that came out of it. But eventually she came up with a list, and in compiling it – surprised herself.

1. Had the courage to get out of an abusive relationship.
2. Started to rebuild the confidence that my partner had been undermining for years. Now I know that it wasn't my fault.
3. Made a brave decision to leave my husband because I was putting my son first. I love my son and I want what is best for him.

So, take a look back at the 'failure' you have identified in your own life. Focus on it and write down three positive learning outcomes that have come from that negative experience.

1.

2.

3.

Action

Focus on making today a day full of learning experiences for you and your children. You can do this for them. Take 'fail' out of your vocabulary and theirs and commit to being an excellent role model for them.

Commit to talking and thinking in terms of why things 'will be successful' rather than focusing on the reasons why things are 'likely to go wrong'.

Think about how you handle the situation when your children declare, 'I can't do this'. Think of all the different ways that you can turn that 'I can't' into an 'I can' for them.

Replace 'I can't' with 'I can' and help them to propel themselves forward for the rest of their lives.

DAY 7: CONFIDENCE UPDATE

It's the end of the week, so you should be feeling much more confident in all sorts of different ways by now. This chapter is a challenging and fulfilling one. By completing each of the daily exercises, you will be noticing significant differences in the way you feel about yourself and how your children feel about themselves – building that all-important confidence from within, for all of you.

Your boosted confidence will be having an impact in every area of your life and in every relationship. Remember, the more frequently you focus on reasons to be confident, the more confident you will feel.

You have now reached day seven of your action plan and by completing each of the daily exercises you will have come a long way in establishing a strategy that will help you.

By now you have:

■ Discovered that if you think you can, you can. You are smiling more and committed to spending more time focusing on reasons to be confident rather than to lack confidence.
■ Developed a practical plan to turbo-boost your own confidence.
■ Removed confidence drains and learned to re-frame apparently negative comments.
■ Created a strategy to boost your confidence as a parent.
■ Committed to creating children 'who can' rather than children 'who can't', and identified ways to do this.
■ Decided that failing isn't an option – for you or your children.

■ Which of the confidence-building skills have you most enjoyed working on over the past week?
■ What positive impact has this had on your relationship with yourself and your children?

Think about how you felt at the beginning of the week and how you feel today.

■ What has been the biggest challenge for you this week?
■ What is the biggest positive difference in the way you feel today, compared with the feelings you experienced at the beginning of the week?

Read your Parent Achievement Log (see page 291) for this week and recognise all that you have achieved. Take your time and enjoy the feeling of achievement. Focus on the difference you are making to yourself and to your family by thinking and acting positively and taking control of your confidence. You have discovered now that confidence can be boosted from within and by taking small steps you have come a long way in just one week.

Now rank your achievements from one to seven with number one being the achievement that has had the biggest impact on you and your family this week.

1. _____

2. _____

3. _____

4. _____

5. _____

6. _____

7. _____

■ What makes this your biggest achievement of the week?
■ What impact has it had on you?
■ What impact has it had on your relationship with your children?
■ How does that feel?

Action

As children, we often believe that we can do anything, but by the time we become adults, we find we've lost that absolute self-confidence somewhere along the way.

It's important for you to continue to nourish your own needs if you are to continue to grow and develop. So, answer this question for me, *When was the last time you did something for the first time?*

What would you love to do that would excite you and propel you out of your comfort zone?

Prove to yourself that you've got what it takes to do it this week. It may be extremely challenging. You may be scared – but just do it.

chapter nine

feel great
– not guilty –
about being a working parent

DAY 1: FORGET WORK-LIFE BALANCE – ENJOY THE BEST OF BOTH WORLDS

One of the mums I've coached, Sophia, has two energetic toddlers. She works part-time as a manager in the NHS. When I first met her, she was very emotional about the stressful challenges of being a working mother. 'I'm feeling guilty and worried all the time,' she said to me. 'Every day is a struggle for me and I just end up feeling that I fail at both jobs. I'm always tired. I'm failing as a mum and as an employee. I'm trying my best but I do neither job well. On top of that, I've lost sight of the real me. When I'm at work, I'm worrying about what I haven't done at home. When I'm at home, I'm worrying about what I haven't done at work. I used to be a really positive person and have lots of fun but now I seem to be guilty and stressed all the time.'

Sophia's experience is typical. Many working parents fall into the trap of blurring the lines between work and home. It's so easy to do isn't it? When you're at work you are worrying about what you haven't done or need to do at home. When you're at home, you're worrying about what you should have done or need to do at work. The problem with this frame of mind is that it increases your stress levels in both places. You end up spending a lot of time worrying about things, but you're not in the right place to do anything about them. You dwell on the negative rather than channelling all your energy into successfully doing the job in hand.

Guilt is the most powerful negative feeling that the majority of working parents struggle with. For working parents, guilt can have a significant negative effect. On some days it can seem that you feel guilty about everything. Feelings of guilt can pervade your family and work life. When you are at work, you can feel guilty about leaving the children. When you are with the children, you can feel guilty about being negative with them and shouting. This is especially true of the early mornings and evenings when you are with your children but feeling stressed and tired. Either you're rushing to get everyone out of the house or it is the end of a challenging day at work.

The focus for this week is on how to succeed as a working parent. As every mum and dad will appreciate, all parents are working parents, it's just that some are in paid employment and some aren't. In this chapter, we're going to focus on parents in full or part-time employment. However, as all parents are very busy people I'm sure you'll find lots of useful ideas in this chapter to help reduce your stress and boost your energy – even if you're not in paid employment.

The first step this week is to stop saying that much-used term, 'work-life balance'. I think it's very unhelpful. It suggests there is bound to be tension between your life and your work and that if you're doing anything in one of those areas, something has to give in the other. I want you to aim for 'the best of both worlds' instead. If you go out to work and you are a parent, focus on creating strategies that will help you to get the most out of both of those important roles. Come up with creative ways of doing what you want to do, and enjoy the challenge of combining parenthood with a career.

The key to achieving this lies with you. Of course, being a working parent brings with it all sorts of challenges, but there are lots of bonuses, too. Instead of dwelling on the negative feelings you have, focus on all the positive feelings it brings. As we know, negative feelings are extremely powerful, especially when you're constantly sending messages to yourself and nurturing that negative inner parent. So, commit to looking for the positive this week and build yourself up instead of undermining yourself.

Over the next seven days, we will explore ways of helping you to make changes in the time you spend with your family. We will also look at specific strategies that you can adopt at work. All the actions will have a positive effect at home and at work. This week is all about achieving what you want to achieve in the time you have.

The starting point for our journey is to focus on you and to get to the core of what will help you move forward as you combine these two rewarding, challenging and important roles in life. The stress you feel in combining parenthood and work is not caused by your children or your job, it is to do with your frame of mind and your response to your family and your work. Remember, in order to reduce stress and boost energy, it is important to be positive and take control. Focus on all the reasons why you want to make your role as a working parent work – not on the reasons that make this difficult. Only this can help you move forwards. It will have a significant impact on you, on your family, and on your job. It's a win, win, win situation.

Top 10 Working Parent Challenges	Never	Occasionally	Often
At work, feelings of guilt about being away from your children.			
At home, feelings of guilt about being negative when you are with your children (for example, shouting and being impatient).			
Feelings of guilt about leaving work at set times because of family commitments.			
Reduced confidence in yourself and the way your colleagues perceive you.			
Lack of 'me time'.			
Difficulty 'switching off' (thinking about work when at home and home when at work).			
Carrying out work tasks in 'family time' (for example, logging on to email, creating 'to do' lists, making or taking work phone calls).			
Struggling with getting everything done in the time available, both at home and at work.			
Dealing with practical family problems that impact on work (such as child care and illness).			
Lack of energy impacting negatively on you and your relationships.			

Take a look at the table on page 205 outlining the challenges that many working parents struggle with. Over the years, I've coached hundreds of working parents and have found that these are the issues that are raised most frequently in parent coaching sessions.

Focus on how often you feel that each of these challenges affects you: never, occasionally or often.

Take your time to focus on each of the 10 challenges. While you have been thinking about these, perhaps you have identified a challenge that isn't included in the list above. It may be something that is unique to your situation, drains your energy and boosts your stress levels. If so, include it.

What are the three biggest challenges for you as a working parent?

```
┌──────────────────────────────────────────────────────┐
│  1.                                                    │
│                                                        │
└──────────────────────────────────────────────────────┘
```

```
┌──────────────────────────────────────────────────────┐
│  2.                                                    │
│                                                        │
└──────────────────────────────────────────────────────┘
```

```
┌──────────────────────────────────────────────────────┐
│  3.                                                    │
│                                                        │
└──────────────────────────────────────────────────────┘
```

■ What makes you choose those challenges?
■ What is the negative impact that they have on your life at the moment?
■ What impact do they have on your relationship with your children?
■ How would you feel if you could make positive changes in these key areas?
■ What difference will it make to you and your family if you successfully reduce your stress, boost your energy and achieve the best of both worlds?

Action

It's important to act today. The longer you let the negative 'guilt gremlin' hang around, the more powerful he'll become. The more time you spend feeling guilty, the more guilty you will become. It's a waste of your valuable time. For working parents, the 'guilt gremlin' is extremely powerful. He knows how to make you feel as bad as possible, especially at those times when you're feeling at your most vulnerable. But he can only do this because you let him. You give him his power. He's only as strong as you allow him to be. Don't try to be the perfect parent – there's no such thing. Do the best you can.

How does feeling guilty benefit you or your family? It doesn't. When you're with your children, be the happiest mum or dad you can possibly be and they'll feel valued. Enjoy being a parent.

Cuddle your children today and focus on all the reasons that you have to feel good – not guilty – about being a parent.

- What do you love most about them?
- What do they love about you?
- What qualities make you a great mum or dad?
- What do you enjoy most about your job?
- What do you find most rewarding about successfully combining parenthood and work?
- How does it strengthen your relationship with your children?

Say your answers out loud.

When your 'guilt gremlin' appears, don't listen to him. Focus on all the reasons you have to feel great – not guilty – about being a working parent.

It's really important that we acknowledge our achievements as parents. Each day I want you to make a note of your biggest achievement (see Parent Achievement Log, page 291). It may be something you achieve when you're carrying out your daily coaching action. Or it may be something that just happens in the course of the day and you think to yourself, 'Yes! That was great!' You decide what is significant for you.

DAY 2: FOCUS ON FAMILY OR WORK – NOT BOTH

Many working parents increase their stress levels on a daily basis because they get into the habit of diluting their energy and focus. When they are at work, they think about family issues. When they are at home, they think about work issues. As a parent, you're so used to thinking about 101 things at once and creating never-ending 'to do' lists that your mind is constantly adding to them.

Take the first step towards reducing your stress levels by focusing on this issue. In the short-term, thinking about lots of things at the same time may make you feel better because you are multi-tasking. You may think that this means you are actually being extremely efficient. In fact, your time and energy will be much better spent if you focus on specific tasks in hand – meeting the challenges and enjoying the rewards.

It takes courage and commitment to be a mum or dad at home and an employee at work and to be very clear about where the line is drawn. You'll be happier and achieve more if you focus on specific roles. Be the best parent you can possibly be at home and the best employee you can be at work.

A little while ago, I was coaching Teresa, a mum with twins, Billy and Alexander. She worked four days a week for a big company and was totally stressed. Teresa enjoyed her job and got lots out of it but found being a mum incredibly stressful and so she really wasn't enjoying it. Evenings and days off were a nightmare. She found one of her twins particularly challenging. Teresa broke down in tears as she confessed to me that she shouted at him a lot and was constantly telling him she wished he was more like his brother. She told me she felt she just didn't have what it takes to be a mum.

I asked Teresa to focus on what happened when she was at home and to identify any particular hot spots for her and the family. I asked her to focus on what it was that made the evenings and days off so stressful. She identified the root of her problem. It wasn't the twins. It was herself and the way she felt.

Teresa said that she often thought about work when she was at home. She struggled to make the four days work for her. When she was at home with the children, her mind would often be creating work 'to do' lists. She found it impossible to switch off. She would often do work-related tasks at home, trying desperately to squeeze in just a few extra minutes here and there. I'm sure that you will be able to identify with Teresa's challenge. Many working mums say to me that part-time work is great – in theory. But the reality is that they usually end up trying to fit five days' work into three or four days. That definitely doesn't work and causes a huge amount of stress for them, both at work and at home.

I asked Teresa to keep a diary over one week and to make a note of all the work-related tasks she did at home. She was amazed at how much time and energy she was actually investing in work when she was supposed to be a mum to Billy and Alexander. Once she'd written everything down in black and white, she discovered that far from a few minutes here and there, she was devoting a significant chunk of her 'family' time to work.

Her list for seven days included all of the following:

- Thinking about work – every evening and days off.
- Talking to her partner about stress at work – daily.
- Writing work 'to do' lists or creating mental work 'to do' lists – four times.
- Logging on to work emails – daily, in the evenings, on days off and at weekends.
- Taking work phone calls at home – three times.
- Phoning work on her day off – once.

Teresa said that it was really no surprise she was struggling at home because her mind just wasn't on it. She was fixed in the pattern of worrying about work, even when there was no reason to, because she could do nothing about it anyway.

I asked Teresa to prioritise the work tasks she was doing at home and identify the one that was having the greatest negative impact on her frame of mind. She knew the answer very quickly – logging on to her work emails. Teresa confessed that she just wanted to make sure that she was always 'up to speed' and that meant logging on to the work email from her home computer. She didn't want to go in on Monday and have any nasty surprises to deal with.

A few years ago, this would not have been an issue for Teresa because so few people had computers at home. Parents couldn't be tempted to work at home in the way they do now. The map of the working world has changed dramatically and this brings challenges for all working parents. The same is true of mobile phones. If we allow it, we can end up on call 24 hours a day. But remember, the answer lies within your control. Situations become stressful and energy dips when the computer or mobile phone takes control of your life. You can control them. You can switch them on or you can switch them off. The decision is yours – not theirs.

Teresa would often log on to her work emails in the evenings when the twins had gone to bed. She admitted that this didn't help her to feel less stressed. It just made her think about everything she had to do at the office the next day. Sometimes she'd see emails that she wanted to act on but could do nothing about. She'd much rather be soaking in a hot bath or taking time to read her daily newspaper. Reading it was a real treat for her. But there was never time to do it in the morning and often she never did get to read it. But Teresa would also try to log on while the twins were playing together. She thought she could just take a couple of minutes for a quick look, but she said this was extremely stressful too. She really could-n't concentrate on the emails because she could hear the children. She was often extremely irritable with the twins if they interrupted her when they wanted her attention. She'd often end up losing control and shouting at them when all they really wanted was to spend time with their mum.

I asked Teresa what she wanted to do about this and she came up with her own three-point action plan.

1. Commit to not logging on to work emails from home for seven days.
2. Commit to not answering work mobile phone when it rang but listen to messages and only call in if there was an absolute emergency. Ask her colleagues to call only in an emergency.
3. Commit to reading the paper each evening when the children have gone to bed instead of logging on to the computer. This would help me to wind down at the end of a busy day.

Teresa achieved this. She said it was extremely scary but very liberating because she began to feel she was back in control of her life again. She had a fantastic long weekend with the twins – no emails and no phone calls – and really felt she had got back in touch with the fun of being a mum. What's more, when she spoke to her line manager and team about what she was planning to do, so that they called only on urgent matters, they were really supportive. Not only did she have a great time with the family, but she said that when she went into work on Monday morning she felt energised and raring to go. She was more positive and more creative with all her work tasks. A great result.

As working parents we all have different challenges in terms of switching off. You may be saying, 'Well that's all right for her but I couldn't possibly do it in my job, it's just not practical.' Well, let me share this with you. It is possible. This is your life and the decision is yours. Remember that Teresa found that reducing the time she spent thinking about work when she was at home didn't have a negative impact on her family or her career. By taking control, she felt less stressed, more energetic and performed better in both roles. If you don't try it and really work at finding a way to make this happen, you'll never know. What I'd like you to do is to focus on this for the next seven days. Be an employee at work and a parent at home. See what a great difference it makes to you in both areas of your life, and I'm sure you'll decide to continue once the week is up.

If you keep on doing what you are doing, you will keep on getting what you are getting and feeling how you are feeling. Commit today to taking positive action and taking control.

WORK-LIFE STRESS SCORE

Make a list of any work-related tasks that you have carried out in family time over the past week. The family time may be early mornings, evenings, days off or weekends.

Remember to include:

- Thinking about work.
- Doing work tasks.
- Waking up in the night worrying about work.

- Talking about work.
- Writing work 'to do' lists.
- Creating mental work 'to do' lists.
- Logging on to work emails from home.
- Taking work phone calls or texts at home.
- Phoning work or sending texts on days off.
- Getting to work early, or leaving work late to finish work tasks (and losing family time in the process).

Of the 10 tasks listed above, how many have you done over the past seven days? What is your work-life stress score out of 10? Circle one number below.

1   2   3   4   5   6   7   8   9   10

Action

I want you to focus on your two roles – as parent and as employee. For the next week, I want you to commit to keeping them separate. This may be a challenge but you can do it and I know that it will boost your quality of life.

When you are at home, focus on being the best parent you can possibly be. When you are at work, focus on being the best employee you can possibly be. When you are at home, concentrate on your family and don't let work issues take up your time. This week, spend less time worrying about what you haven't done or need to do, and more time doing it.

Focus on your work-life stress score and the work-related tasks that you carry out at home. In which one of them would making changes have the greatest positive impact on your family life and on your relationship with your children? Remember that you are in control. Choose one of the work-related tasks and come up with a positive action plan for the next seven days – and stick to it. You may decide not to log on to the computer, to leave work on time, or not to talk about work at home. You decide – and do it.

Commit to the challenge and tell anyone who needs to know so that they can support you.

DAY 3:
BE POSITIVE ABOUT CHILD CARE

One of the huge challenges that working parents, especially working mums face is feeling guilty about leaving their children. All the working mums I've coached agree that this is the really big one. It can be especially difficult for mums who are leaving their children with a child-minder or in a nursery for the very first time to go back to work.

When mums talk to me about this, they describe their feelings in powerful negative terms that consume their minds and hearts. The reality is that many working parents feel guilty for no real reason other than that they're determined to give themselves a hard time.

In my experience, the majority of working parents invest a lot of time and energy exploring all the child care options available to them so that they can make a great decision about where to leave their child while they are at work. This is because they are passionate about their children and want them to be surrounded by love, compassion, fun – and all those other family values that are important to them.

When you're choosing child care, make a list of the top 10 criteria that you want it to satisfy in an ideal world.

- What values are you looking for?
- How happy are the children there?
- What is the most impressive quality demonstrated by the staff?
- What practical considerations are important?

Think of everything that needs to go on that list. This way you'll know that by choosing an option which meets as many of the criteria as possible, you are making a proactive, considered and excellent child care option. It hasn't just happened.

Don't just look at a few nurseries or child-minders and then choose the best out of those you've seen. Take the time to identify what is important to you and how you're going to decide which of the options are suitable. You may be surprised at the results and find that a nursery or child-minder you'd virtually discounted in your mind actually satisfies more of your criteria than some of the more likely candidates. Be creative and brainstorm as many possible options as you can. It's important that you take the time and space to focus on this because it is a huge decision.

As a parent, you have excellent gut instinct so make sure you use it. Of course, listen to what other parents say, if you want to, but remember that your children are individuals and you are the expert on them, their wants and their needs.

If you feel that you're not in a position to make a choice about child care, perhaps because of financial considerations or logistics, make a list of all the positive skills and qualities demonstrated by the child-minder or the nursery staff. What are the benefits that will come from your children spending time with them?

If you've taken the time to make good decisions about their child care, you have lots of reasons to feel positive about their child care. You've thought about it and made the decision with their best interests at heart.

One of my clients, Jan, was a new mum just back at work. She was feeling dreadfully guilty about being away from Amber, who was just a year old. Jan told me that she really liked her nursery, and the staff were great, but she always felt guilty about leaving Amber there. When Jan thought about her she would cry. She would think about her missing her and wondering why she'd left her there.

Jan was finding her feelings of guilt overwhelming – and no wonder. Her frame of mind was such that she felt bad all the time, not only when she was at work but also when she was with Amber.

If you've made good child-care decisions, you have no reason to feel guilty. Don't let your imagination run riot and convince yourself that your children are spending the day in Alcatraz, desperately trying to escape and wondering what kind of a mother or father would possibly leave them there.

Focus on all the things that your children get out of child care on a daily basis. It's certainly helping them to develop strong social skills and to become independent. There are lots of benefits that come from spending time with adults – other than you – and with other children. What do you like most about the child-minder or nursery? Ask the staff what activities your child enjoys most of all.

Action

Choose a happy photo of your children – a real favourite showing them laughing or smiling. Put it on your desk at work, or in your pocket, somewhere where it is easy for you to take out and look at. When you do think about them in the nursery or with a child-minder, picture them having fun, not being sad. Think about all the positives and imagine them having a wonderful time engaged in their favourite activity. Whenever you start to feel guilty, focus on this image. If your children are laughing and smiling. You can too. Feeling good, not guilty about being a working parent will benefit all of you.

Travelling to and from the nursery or child-minder can be a real guilt trip too. You're either feeling guilty about taking them to the nursery or guilty about feeling tired and stressed and not having enough energy to be the perfect parent. Add the pressure of heavy traffic and this journey can be a nightmare.

Approach your travelling times differently. Instead of wasting time feeling guilty, see the journey through your children's eyes. Make it a big adventure for them. Get into the habit of looking forward to the journey rather than dreading it.

DAY 4:
REDUCE STRESS LEVELS AT WORK

The next step is to focus on effective ways to reduce the stress you feel while you are at work. One of the biggest causes of stress for many parents, especially mums, comes at the end of the day when they're trying to leave work on time to meet important family commitments, such as picking up a child from the nursery.

For women, especially, this kind of stress can be so powerful. I was recently asked to speak at a corporate event. The key speaker was a very senior male manager and he was talking to an audience of women employees. 'The problem with our culture,' he said, 'is that if you are a man and you leave work on time to go to see your son or daughter play football, everyone says, "What a great dad." If you are a mum leaving the office on time to pick up your little one from the nursery or the child-minder, every-one says, "What's wrong? Isn't she committed to the company?" '

I was coaching a client, Tina, recently who struggled with this very issue. Tina said that she had to leave the office punctually every day as the nursery where her toddler, Mattie, spends the day closed promptly at that time. The nursery was very close to her office, which was very convenient, but working late was not an option.

Tina described to me how she felt both during the 30 minutes before she left the office and at the moment when she was actually leaving the office. She described her feelings in very specific detail and the feelings of stress were overwhelming for her. Tina would spend the last half hour constantly telling herself that she should really be staying to do other things as she hadn't finished all her work. She would be constantly apol-ogising to colleagues for the fact that she couldn't attend late meetings because she had to leave work on time. But the worst part of all for her was actually walking out of the office. This was because she was usually the first to leave and she had to walk the length of the room, right past everybody else, busily tapping away at their computers. Every day, Tina felt as though all eyes were on her and that everyone was thinking that she was not up to the job and not working as hard as they were because she was leaving before them. She also felt guilty about working part-time and not being in the office on Fridays.

These feelings of guilt, powerful as they are, are entirely down to you. You let them have this power over you so it is important to develop strategies to reduce that power. This will have a positive impact on every-thing you feel and do, both at work and at home.

I asked Tina to complete a Stress Reduction Wheel, brainstorming any ideas that she could come up with that would help her to feel less stressed during her day in the office and especially when leaving on time to pick up little Mattie from the nursery. The first step was to get her to focus on the positive reasons for being at work and for leaving promptly. This was to motivate her to be creative in her problem solving. The second step was to think of all the practical things that she could do.

This is what her Stress Reduction Wheel looked like:

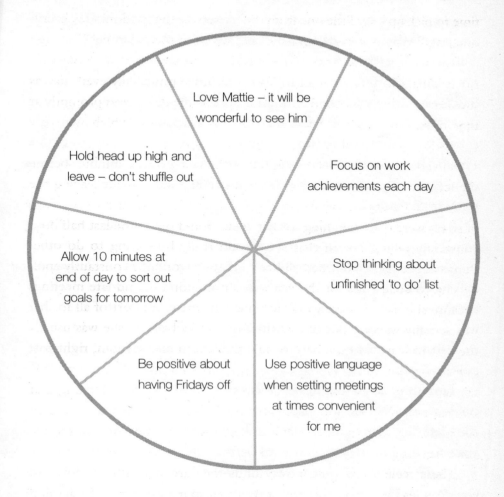

This is how she explained what she'd written in the wheel:

Tina said the most important thing would be to focus on Mattie's face when she picks him up from the nursery, rather than imagine what all her colleagues are thinking. She also wanted to enjoy the journey home with Mattie, rather than be worrying about the work she's left at the office. Tina was in the habit of giving herself a hard time about all the things she'd left on her 'to do' list. She decided that from now on she was going to focus only on what she'd achieved at work that day – and keep a diary of her accomplishments. Not only would this be very affirming for her on a daily basis, but it would also be invaluable for her personal review with her line manager! She also talked about the negative and defensive language she uses at work. Tina felt guilty about leaving the office on time and working only four days a week and this was reflected in her language. This made it stressful whenever she had to arrange meetings. She would say things like, 'I'm afraid I can't do a meeting then as I have to leave at 5.30', or, 'I'm sorry, I'm not in on a Friday so can we do it on another day?' She said that she knew there was absolutely no reason why she should be apologising for leaving work on time or not being there on a Friday (she was paid to work part-time not full-time after all), but she still consistently drew attention to these hot spots – and boosted her stress levels in the process.

Tina drew up her own action plan. Her Stress Reduction Wheel contained seven great ideas that were both practical and easy to implement.

She worked out very specifically what she would say to colleagues and to clients: 'These are the days and times over the next week that I am available for a meeting. Which one would be suitable for you?' She was going to stop drawing attention to the occasions that she wouldn't be available – as the only purpose it served was to increase her feelings of guilt and stress.

Tina also put 10 minutes of 'focus time' into her diary at the end of every afternoon. She found this extremely helpful as it enabled her to complete her achievement diary and gave her the time to set specific goals for the next day. It meant she left the office feeling that her work was under control. This was very different from her usual experience. Usually, she'd be running around madly trying to get everything completed before 5.30pm and leaving the office mid-task and in a state of stress. She'd go out of the door feeling she was leaving an unfinished mess behind her.

Finally, Tina committed to leaving the office with her head held high and to making a point of saying goodbye to her colleagues, rather than shuffling out hoping that they wouldn't notice. She was leaving the office as a positive choice. It was a good decision. She'd done a good day's work and now she was going to focus on being a mum.

The following week, Tina reported back that she felt much less stressed about leaving work and that, actually, her colleagues had been very supportive. She had started to feel really positive as 5.30pm approached, rather than dreading it. Tina also believed that, by changing her attitude and keeping to a simple action plan, she'd improved her motivation and productivity at work. It was interesting that she raised this point. The national charity Parentalk conducted a national survey that showed that nine out of 10 working mothers believed combining career and motherhood had resulted in improved productivity, decision-making and creative problem-solving skills.

By creating her own positive action plan, Tina has taken a significant step as a working mother. Her solution-focused strategy reduced her stress levels so effectively that she was able to enjoy work and home more. She has taken an important step towards achieving **the best of both worlds.**

Action

Complete your own working parent Stress Reduction Wheel overleaf. Brainstorm all the practical ideas that you can try out over the next week to help you to make positive changes that will reduce your stress levels.

Once you have completed the wheel, you will have seven great ways to reduce your stress levels at work over the next seven days. Rank your ideas from one to seven with number one being the idea you would like to put into action first.

1. _____

2. _____

3. _____

4. _____

5. _____

6. _____

STRESS REDUCTION

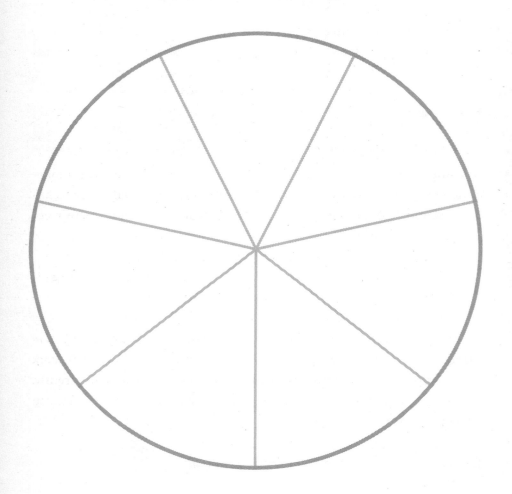

7. _____

Put each of your ideas into your diary and commit to trying them this week
– a day at a time. Life's too short to spend it feeling stressed. Start today to
make small changes to reduce those stress levels. You can do this and it will
bring benefits at work and at home.

DAY 5: BE THE BEST FAMILY MANAGING DIRECTOR POSSIBLE

As a mother or father, you are the managing director of the most important company in the world. Forget multi-national blue chip
organisations. You are responsible for your children – and it doesn't get
any bigger than that.

As managing director of your family, you make important decisions
on a daily basis. You deal with personnel issues, strategy, budgets, organisation, productivity – not to mention crisis management.

Lots of the mums and dads that I coach tell me that they feel very
different at home from the way they feel at work. They're quite separate
worlds and although they may worry about home while they are at work
– and vice versa – they approach the tasks in each world quite differently.

Today, I want you to focus on the greatest skills and qualities that you
take into your job with you.

- What would you identify as your top three?
- What makes you great at your job?

1.

> 2.

> 3.

Focus on what makes these such positive skills and qualities for you. How do they help your performance at work?

Today, I want you to focus on putting those skills into practice at home. You may already be doing this, but today, I want you to boost those skills and qualities with your family.

I was coaching a mum, Selina, who works for a charity. She's a fantastic asset, both to her family and to the organisation. Her role in the charity is to raise its profile and funds so that it can make a difference to homeless young people. Selina has a two-year-old daughter, Marisa, and is expecting her second child. She told me that she'd found the challenge of fitting everything in a real shock to her system. Selina identified the evenings as being the most stressful time for her. From 5pm to 7pm are mad hours in her house. She tried to do loads of things at once and felt constantly tired and stressed.

Selina ranked her top three professional skills as:

1. Effective planner.
2. Project management and strong team-builder.
3. Ability to 'think outside the box'.

I asked Selina how she would approach her evening hot spot if it was a work-related project and how that approach might make a difference at home. She immediately picked up on the fact that at work she has a reputation for being extremely well organised and an effective planner. Selina deals with project management on a daily basis, running a big team and taking responsibility for managing big budgets. It dawned on her, while we were talking, that at home she plays a very different role. She sees herself as being disorganised. With Marisa, she doesn't plan, she reacts to whatever happens in the home. Selina was two quite different people: one at work and one at home. The skills and qualities that helped her to excel in the office flew out the window once she walked through her own front door.

Selina focused on her professional skills and qualities and applied these to the home situation. She drew up a specific timetable for the two 'mad' hours in the evening on her terms and not Marisa's – and stuck to it. She approached the challenge as a motivated project manager and established a routine that worked for the whole family. She had been doing everything herself but now delegated tasks to her husband, Roy, and her in-laws, who came round once a week to have tea with them. They all enjoyed the additional responsibilities – it paid huge dividends with her mother-in-law – and Selina started to enjoy her evenings again.

Selina said she found planning – rather than surviving – extremely liberating. On top of that, she decided that she wanted to energise her home life. At work, she was the human dynamo, but at home she usually felt tired and stressed. On her days off Selina decided to sleep when her toddler sleeps so that she would feel re-energised for the evening shift. She said going to sleep when she was surrounded by things that needed doing was a huge challenge but she's done it and it has made a huge difference. Selina said that in her career, she would always make time to 'think outside the box' so that she was constantly keeping the charity at the cutting edge. At home, she never created the time and space to apply the same principles. She's now committed to managing family life differently and more effectively. She's taken control in a way that is second nature to her in her career.

Action

Take a look at the three key skills and qualities that you have identified as being significant for you in your professional life.

1. _____

2. _____

3. _____

Focus on one specific family hot spot and imagine that you were dealing with this in a work situation. If you were dealing with this particular challenge as a work project, how would you approach it?

It's time to raise your game.

■ How can those skills and qualities help you to be the best managing director your family could possibly have?

If you can excel in those skills at work, you can excel in them at home. They're there just waiting to be used.

■ How would you do things differently from the way you do them now?
■ What difference do you think this would make to you and the family?

The next time your challenging situation arises, deal with it using those key skills and qualities.

DAY 6:
BOOST YOUR ENERGY

I know that you are really going to enjoy today because it's the day you begin to really boost your energy. You'll appreciate by now that an effective way to do this is to face challenges head on and begin to deal with some of the stresses and strains in your life.

Now I want you to think very positive. What can you do during the course of today that will positively boost your energy? I want you to make this so simple for yourself that you can't help but feel healthier and energised. Lack of energy is one of the commonest challenges that working parents face – and it is certainly the commonest complaint I hear in the coaching sessions. So, stop focusing on what's draining your energy and think about what you can do in practical terms to positively boost your energy.

ENERGY RATING

How energetic would you say that you feel on a scale of 1 to 10? A rating of 1 indicates very low energy levels. A rating of 10 indicates extremely high energy levels. Circle the number below that applies to you.

1   2   3   4   5   6   7   8   9   10

■ How would you feel if your energy rating was 10 on a regular basis?
■ How would you know that it was that high?
■ What would you be doing that you aren't doing now?
■ What would be the one most significant positive difference that it would make in your life?

In a moment, I'm going to ask you to complete your own Energy Boosting Wheel, giving a list of everything you can easily do in just one day to boost your energy.

I asked Bea, a working mum, to complete this assignment for me. She's a traffic warden and was finding the public's negative reaction to her extremely draining. I asked her to complete the Energy Boosting Wheel using the following guidelines.

The Energy Boosting Wheel should include:

■ One positive action that you can achieve before you leave for work.
■ One positive action that you can achieve during your working day.
■ One positive action that you can achieve at lunchtime.
■ One positive action that you can achieve on your way to or from work.
■ One positive action that you can achieve in the evening.

My only other stipulation was that Bea needed to think positively and frame her ideas positively, rather than think negatively in terms of what she was giving up. The Energy Boosting Wheel was to be filled with energy boosters that worked for her. They had to be easy, so that it was possible to do them all in one day.

Here's her Energy Boosting Wheel:

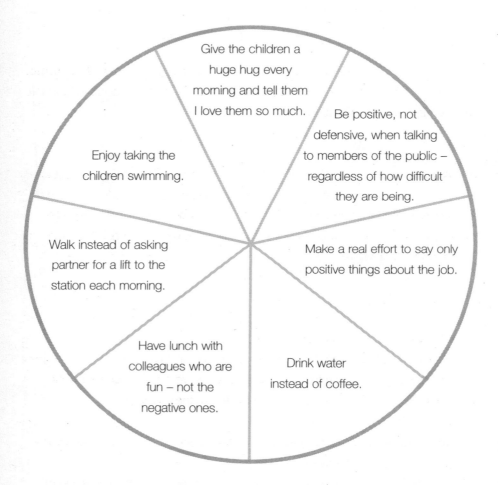

Easy. Bea managed to achieve them all in just one day. She said she felt higher energy levels from the time she woke up. Instead of focusing on the negative aspects of the day, she was boosting energy by thinking positive and taking positive action. Her day was within her control. Bea's ideas were all simple things really, but each of them provided a good energy booster. Her favourite was giving the children a big hug.

She realised that sometimes she just didn't get around to doing it. Her commitment to being positive with members of the public made her feel much better and produced some surprisingly positive results with her clients. She said that the swimming was an interesting one. When she got in from work, she really didn't feel like going out again – but she went anyway. Once at the pool, they all had a terrific time and she felt more energetic not less. It made eating a healthy dinner even more tempting!

The energy boosters made a difference to her at work and at home. It wasn't just her who reaped the benefits, so did her colleagues, the public, and her family at home.

Action

Complete your own Energy Boosting Wheel overleaf. Remember, the key is to make everything in it so simple that you can do it today with very little effort. Focus on those actions you can take that will positively boost your energy, rather than about what you are giving up!

Your Energy Boosting Wheel should include:

- One positive action that you can achieve before you leave for work.
- One positive action that you can achieve during your working day.
- One positive action that you can achieve at lunchtime.
- One positive action that you can achieve on your way to or from work.
- One positive action that you can achieve in the evening.

You need to be able to integrate your ideas into your everyday life. That way, they're much more likely to happen.

Then commit to turbo-boosting your energy by completing all seven of the actions that you have listed over the next seven days.

ENERGY BOOSTING

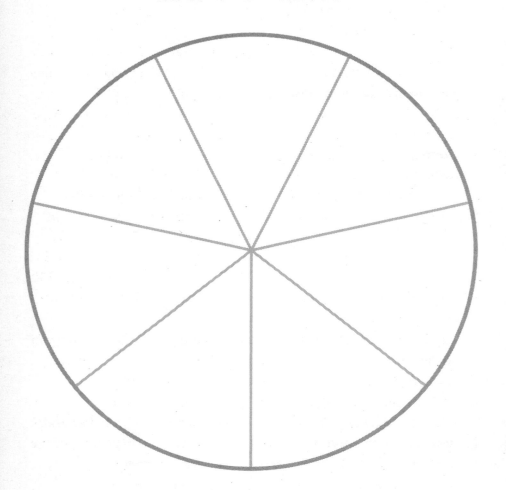

DAY 7:
BEST OF BOTH WORLDS UPDATE

You have now reached day seven of your action plan and by completing each of the daily exercises you will have come a long way in establishing an effective strategy that will help you as a working parent to get the best of both worlds – at home and at work.

By now you have:

- Started to feel great – not guilty – about being a working parent and are beginning to enjoy the best of both worlds.
- Reduced stress by committing to focusing on work at work and on family at home.
- Created a plan to enable you to feel positive about child care.
- Reduced stress levels at work.
- Committed to being the best family managing director possible.
- Developed a daily strategy to boost your energy.

At the beginning of the week, I asked you to consider the top 10 challenges that face working parents. Take a look at the table on page 230 and indicate in which areas you believe you have made positive moves forward this week.

Think about how you felt at the beginning of the week and how you feel today.

- What has been the biggest challenge for you this week?
- What is the biggest positive difference in the way you feel today compared with the feelings you experienced at the beginning of the week?
- How far do you think you have come on your journey?
- Are you beginning to feel that you are enjoying the best of both worlds?

Top 10 Working Parent Challenges	I HAVE MADE A POSITIVE MOVE FORWARD IN THIS AREA
At work, feelings of guilt about being away from your children.	
At home, feelings of guilt about being negative when you are with your children (for example, shouting and being impatient).	
Feelings of guilt about leaving work at set times because of family commitments.	
Reduced confidence in yourself and the way your colleagues perceive you.	
Lack of 'me time'.	
Difficulty 'switching off' (thinking about work when at home and home when at work).	
Carrying out work tasks in 'family time' (for example, logging on to email, creating 'to do' lists, making or taking work phone calls).	
Struggling with getting everything done in the time available, both at home and at work.	
Dealing with practical family problems that impact on work (such as child care and illness).	
Lack of energy impacting negatively on you and your relationships.	

Action

Read your Parent Achievement Log (see page 291) for this week and recognise all that you have accomplished. Take your time and enjoy the feeling of achievement. Focus on the difference you are making to yourself and to your family by thinking and acting positively and taking control of how you feel about being a working parent. You're successfully combining two of the most challenging, rewarding and important roles in your life. Well done. You're achieving a huge amount on a daily basis.

Now rank your achievements from one to seven with number one being the achievement that has had the biggest impact on you and your family this week.

1. _____

2. _____

3. _____

4. _____

5. _____

6. _____

7. _____

■ What makes this your biggest achievement of the week?

■ What impact has it had on you?

■ What impact has it had on your relationship with your children?

■ How does that feel?

chapter ten

rise to the challenge

of your family budget

Paula was one of my clients. She was bringing up her three-year-old, Tiffany, on her own. She had a job at a local school that helped bring in some money to make ends meet. Paula said she felt stressed and anxious all the time. Money was her biggest worry. She wanted to give her daughter the best start in life possible – especially as Tiffany's father wasn't around. Some days, Paula felt so down about life, she didn't even get dressed.

Within six months of parent coaching, Paula had transformed her family life. She was an incredibly creative woman but she'd done nothing with her skills for over 20 years. She decided to follow her passion and start her own successful business, working on unique art commissions for parents. Word spread quickly and she was much in demand. She could fit all her work around her family commitments and was regularly earning more in one week than she'd earned in months at the school. What was the key? A win on the lottery? An inheritance? A bank loan?

No, the key wasn't money. It was Paula herself. Paula is a talented woman, she'd just forgotten to believe in herself. Once she did, there was absolutely no stopping her. She was now in a position to buy things for Tiffany that she'd only dreamed of before. I asked Paula to tell me what her most significant gift for Tiffany had been since the business had taken off. She only thought for a couple of seconds. 'Me', she said. 'Tiffany has got her mum back.'

This week, we are going to take a close look at the challenge of the family budget. Now, whenever I mention those words in my seminars, I can see by the faces of all the mothers and fathers in the audience that this whole subject makes their hearts sink. You know just how much it can cost to raise a family. Everything's so expensive – or is it?

Over the next seven days, we're going to change your view of money and take control of your purse strings in a way that you've never managed before. By the end of the week, you'll have developed the frame of mind that will not only reduce any anxieties about money that you may have but will also help you to boost your income. How's that for a bargain?

To begin with, I want you to focus on the word 'money'. There, we've said it. Perhaps, like lots of my clients you don't even like to talk about it. Budgeting is a necessary evil that's part of family life. So face up to it.

- What does that word mean to you?
- What does it make you think of?
- Where do your beliefs about money come from?
- How do you really feel about it?

If you want to reduce the stress and boost your energy where finance is concerned, you need to begin by ensuring that you have a positive attitude to money. For many people, this can be a real challenge because their attitudes have grown many years and are extremely deep-rooted. It's also very common for your financial anxieties to increase significantly when you have a child. It is easy to understand why this happens. Raising a family brings new expenses; you are no longer responsible just for yourself, but also for a family. Suddenly, the stakes seem much higher.

Many mums and dads that I have worked with over the years feel stressed and under pressure because they 'never have enough money'. On a scale of 1 to 10, how stressed do you feel about money – or the lack of it? A rating of 1 indicates a low level of stress. A rating of 10 indicates a high level of stress. Circle the number below that applies to you.

1   2   3   4   5   6   7   8   9   10

The first step is to look at any negative attitudes you have to money and really get to grips with the impact they're having on your life. The more time and energy you spend worrying about money, the more anxious you will feel. It's a vicious circle and you have to break it. You're reinforcing the message that you're constantly sending out to other people and to yourself. Without spending or saving a penny, you are powerfully reinforcing the financial anxieties you are feeling and they are getting stronger and stronger.

How often over the past week have you said something negative about money to yourself – or to somebody else? You may have thought that you don't have enough money, or you can't afford to buy something, or how different life would be if you had more money. It may be the sinking feeling you get when a bill comes in, or a general concern about your lack of control over family finances.

■ How many times over the past week have you experienced negative thoughts about money? Circle the one that applies.

Never   Occasionally   Fairly Often   Frequently

If you are having negative feelings more often than positive feelings, then money is a dictator in your life and is having a powerful limiting effect.

■ How many times over the past week have you experienced positive feelings about money? You may have kept the thoughts to yourself, or you may have voiced them to somebody else. Think about this for a moment. We don't normally associate money with positive feelings unless we win some money or have a pay rise. Circle the one that applies

Never   Occasionally   Fairly Often   Frequently

If you are having positive feelings more often than negative feelings, then money is a liberator and is having a powerful effect that gives you freedom in your life.

■ Is money a dictator or a liberator in your life?

Remember, the more you give time and space to negative thoughts, the more you increase your worries about finance. The more you worry, the more you will worry. And in itself, worrying will do absolutely nothing to change the situation. On the contrary, it will undermine your confidence to take control and make you feel less able to deal with the situation. If you are happy with your life and feeling positive then you are much more likely to be successful in whatever you do.

■ How committed are you to transforming money from dictator to liberator in your life?
■ When you succeed in doing this, what difference will it make to you?
■ How will you feel?

Action

Focus on your relationship with your children.

■ What positive impact has this relationship had on you?
■ How has it helped you to grow stronger as a person?
■ What's the best thing about your special bond with your children?
■ What role does money play in helping you to acquire the quality of relationship that you enjoy as a parent?
■ If you were putting a price on the value of your relationship with your children, what figure would you assign to it?
■ How much is that relationship worth to you? £_____

Today, I want you to focus on having only positive thoughts about money and not negative ones. See how far you can get through the day. The way forward is to have a positive frame of mind. The first step to freedom is to reduce the power that money worry or stress has over you. Then you can move forwards and make positive changes in your life. If you're tempted to have a negative thought, just think about the value of that special relationship you have with your children. You'll feel richer straight away.

It's really important that we acknowledge our achievements as parents. Each day I want you to make a note of your biggest achievement (see Parent Achievement Log, page 291). It may be something you achieve when you're carrying out your daily coaching action. Or it may be something that just happens in the course of the day and you think to yourself, 'Yes! That was great!' You decide what is significant for you.

DAY 2:
START YOUR LIFE BANK BALANCE

I want you to begin today by going on a spending spree – and it will cost you nothing at all. Today, we're going to focus on the value of family life and not the cost.

If you were given all the money in the world and you could spend it on absolutely anything that you wanted, what would be on your shopping list? When I run seminars on this subject, it's not material belongings that parents long for, it's positive and powerful feelings. There are lots of feelings that crop up again and again.

One of my clients, Cathryn, is a very well paid advertising executive. She commands a very impressive salary. Money – or the lack of it – has never been an issue for her. She spends her money on what she wants. I asked her to complete her Feeling Shopping Wheel and this is what it looked like:

Another of my clients, Diana, completed the same exercise. She's a full-time mum at home. Here's her Feeling Shopping Wheel:

As you can see, their lives are very different but there are lots of similarities in the goals they are looking for in life.

Now I want you to complete your own ideal Feeling Shopping Wheel opposite. Remember you can buy anything you want – so choose well.

Once you have completed the exercise, take a look at each of the feelings in turn and imagine what your life will be like if you have this feeling in abundance. You may already have it in your life, in which case imagine having more of it in every way. Now rank those feelings from one to seven with number one being the feeling that would be top of your shopping list without a doubt.

1. _____

2. _____

3. _____

4. _____

FEELING SHOPPING

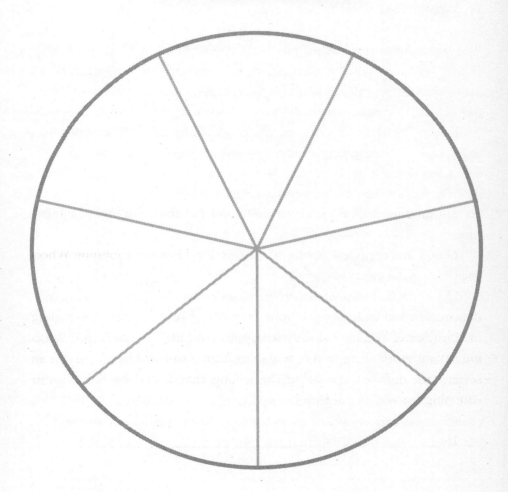

5. _____

6. _____

7. _____

■ What is your number one feeling?

The bad news is that money can't buy you that feeling. The good news is that you can create it yourself without spending any money. We all know the phrase, 'money can't buy you happiness' – and it's true. There are lots of stories in the media every week that demonstrate this well. Money can't buy you happiness. You might think it can. The reason you think that is because you want to boost happiness in your life and your focus for doing that is money. But actually, if you are happy without money, you're likely to be happy with money.

If you are unhappy without money, you're likely to be unhappy with money.

If you are confident without money, you're likely to be confident with money.

If you lack confidence without money, you're likely to lack confidence with money.

Of course, money can buy you things that you enjoy – perhaps a house, a holiday, a car, a dishwasher, toys for your children. They're all material acquisitions. The impact they have on the way you feel is up to you. Feelings will be much more powerful acquisitions and can help you reduce stress and boost energy in the long term. This is you we are talking about – not the things that you buy or own.

Action

Today, I want you to focus on the value of everything you currently have in your life. If you are constantly in pursuit of something you don't yet have, you're unlikely ever to feel really satisfied.

Today, focus only on what you do have in your life. Imagine that you have a bank of life. Every time you feel good today, deposit that positive feeling in your bank of life. You can choose what you bank. It may be the feeling you get when your child says a new word, or you share a cuddle, smile, make time to play, you say you love your child – anything that makes you feel good and glad to be alive.

At the end of the day, take a look at that life bank balance. Imagine you have the statement in front of you.

■ What did you bank today?
■ Think about everything you have on your list. How does that feel?

Be very clear, you are a wealthy person. You have all of this – everything that money can't buy.

DAY 3: TAKE CONTROL OF THE PURSE STRINGS

So far this week you have made an important start to your journey. Every day that you focus on the positive and reduce the power of the negative will help you to move forward with your life. By now, you will be feeling more positive about the value of your family life – rather than the cost of it.

Today, I want you to look at the practicalities of taking control of the family purse strings. When it comes to dealing with the family finances, it can be the feeling of lacking control that increases stress and reduces the energy you have to deal with that stress. We've been working on your frame of mind. Now it is time to get practical and take control of family finances. I want you to focus on identifying your financial energy drains and begin to think of some small ways in which you can deal with them. We're going to break the big picture down into achievable steps. In order to move forwards, I want you to stop wasting time worrying about finance and start investing time in taking action.

On a scale of 1 to 10, how much do you feel you are in control of your finances at the moment? A rating of 1 indicates a low level of control and a rating of 10 indicates a high level of control. Circle the number that applies.

$$1 \quad 2 \quad 3 \quad 4 \quad 5 \quad 6 \quad 7 \quad 8 \quad 9 \quad 10$$

What single thing would you need to achieve in order to move your score half a point up the scale towards the 10? Remember, it needs to be something you can do that is within your control. If it is outside your control, you do not have the power to change it.

It doesn't matter what your financial situation is at the moment. It is all relative. One person's poverty is another person's wealth. What is important is that you take control of the family finances. There may be factors outside of your control, such as divorce, interest rates or redundancy. You can't do anything about them. What you can control is your response to them. You can either worry and do nothing, and be paralysed with fear, or you can commit to rising to the challenge of the family budget and find a way to move forwards – one small step at a time.

The whole area of family finances can sometimes feel so overwhelming that you just don't feel up to dealing with any of it. I've worked with clients in all sorts of financial and family situations who say they don't have the time or energy to make the changes that will help them reduce their worries. But if you keep on doing what you are doing, you will keep on getting what you are getting. The choice is yours.

The reason that most people feel stressful about their family finances is that they know the problem is running out of control. These people are being controlled by their finances, rather than vice versa. How can that possibly happen? Well, it's very easily done. You need to believe that you can control your finances. By bringing all the issues about money within your control, you will be able to reduce your stress levels. There are some things you cannot change. But there are lots of things you can. Take your journey one step at a time.

One of my clients, Maria, was recently divorced. She has two children, aged three and five. She was desperately worried about money and the family. She repeated the same mantra again and again, 'I'm so worried, there just isn't enough to go round. I don't know how we'll manage.' I asked Maria to focus on what life would be like if she was able to manage financially and how different her life would be from how it is now.

Yet Maria had no idea just how much additional finance she would need in order to manage. She just had this overwhelming sense of panic that she wasn't coping – financially and emotionally. She was spending so much time feeling anxious that she'd stopped enjoying the children. Maria also said that once she was in debt, she carried on spending after a while because the money didn't seem real yet the debt kept growing bigger.

Let's start right at the beginning. You need to know the facts. That way, you are fully informed about the situation and you can make good decisions to move forwards. The unknown in any area will fuel your fears.

I asked Maria to complete her Family Finance Actions Wheel. I asked her to include in the wheel a list of all the measures that she could take that would help her bring her finances back under control instead of experiencing the roller-coaster ride that she's on at the moment.

This is what her wheel looked like:

I then asked her to rank her top three actions – the ones she'd like to focus on most this week. Here is her list:

1. Open bank statements and bills.
2. Stop using credit cards.
3. Find out about child care for Tom (three) so I can get back to work.

Maria set to work. The bank statements and bills were a huge drain. She'd even got to the stage where she wasn't opening them but just leaving them in a pile. They were there in the kitchen, a constant reminder that her finances were out of control. She started a finance file and put everything in order. The next step was to stop using credit cards. By her own admission, she was using them to buy things for herself or the children that weren't essential. The credit cards were controlling her instead of her controlling them. She decided the best way to ensure she stopped using them was to cut them up. Maria said it was the most liberating thing she's ever done. She said she felt the power surge back into her body as she took control. Finally, she started to find out what support was available for three-year-old Tom. Maria wanted to do paid work, not only to generate income but also because she believed it would give her back the confidence and self-esteem that had been damaged by the divorce. She hadn't given a job much thought before but now that she focused on it she knew she wanted to find a way to do it. She asked a friend to look after Tom for one morning while she surfed the net and phoned around. Maria found out that she could get financial support to help with Tom's nursery place. This was the lifeline she needed. It meant he would be looked after in a lovely nursery and she would have some time and space to get her life back on track. She reported that a huge weight of guilt was lifted from her. She'd got into the habit of getting bad tempered with the children every time she talked about money and had to tell them she couldn't afford to buy things. Maria found that it helped to talk to them calmly and explain about the value of things and what she could afford. It was a good lesson for them to learn and helped her deal very effectively with her own feelings of guilt at not being able to buy everything they wanted. She was taking control.

When Maria came to me, I offered to coach her free of charge but she said 'no'. She said that she couldn't afford much but she valued the coaching so much each week because it was really helping her get back in control of her life. She paid me a small amount each week – and it was great to work with her. She was one of the most committed clients I have ever had. Money can't buy you the commitment you need to succeed. Over the months, Maria changed her life completely. She sold the family home in London and moved to Dorset where she now works for a local charity dedicated to supporting families in challenging situations. Her financial situation has been transformed – not by any lottery win, but because she took the time to make positive changes that impacted on her life. She took one step at a time, taking herself and her family on an amazing journey. And she still has lots to look forward to.

Action

Today, I want you to focus on what you want to achieve as far as your finances are concerned. Think about how you feel now, and how you would like to feel. Imagine what that life would be like and what changes you need to make to achieve it.

Take the first step towards achieving it.

Complete your Family Finance Actions Wheel overleaf.

In your wheel, write down all the actions you can take that will help you deal with your financial energy drains and enable you to move forwards. Take a look at your wheel and rank your ideas from one to seven with number one being the one that you want to do immediately.

1. _____

2. _____

3. _____

4. _____

FAMILY FINANCE ACTIONS

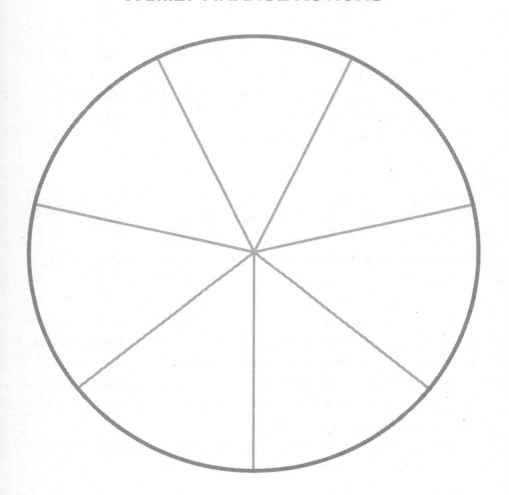

5. _____

6. _____

7. _____

You now have seven great ideas to put into action. Put each one of them into your diary and focus on them, one every day, for the next seven days. By this time next week, you will feel that you have made significant progress and have started to reduce your stress levels by getting back in control.

DAY 4: TEACH YOUR CHILDREN THE VALUE – NOT THE PRICE

By this stage in the week, you will be beginning to feel a real shift in your approach to money and this will impact on every area of your life.

So, today is a good day to take stock and think about the lessons you are teaching your children about value and cost. As we said before, many of us grow up with all sorts of anxieties and fears about money. They can be so deep-rooted that they paralyse us in adult life.

As parents, we often spend lots of time talking about how we want our children to know what's really important in life. And that money isn't the be all and end all.

Often, as you may now be starting to realise, there is a gap between where we are and where we want our children to be. We want them to believe one thing, but often the example we set conveys a quite different message. Remember, many of the important things in life are caught – not taught.

Many parents feel guilty about saying 'no' to their children. Don't feel guilty about saying 'no' – you are teaching them a valuable lesson. Getting into the habit of buying them something, no matter how small, every time you go into a shop is expensive for you and unhelpful for them.

It's important that when you say 'no', you mean it and that your children know you mean it. Children can be very persistent. If they think that if they keep on and on at you that you will crack eventually they'll just carry on doing it. Well, wouldn't you? Talk to your children about your reasons for saying 'no' – explain your decision to them. Don't bargain with them. Be firm and consistent. Help them to understand the message that money doesn't make the world go round and that a 'treat' really is a 'treat'.

If you could teach your children one thing about what is valuable in life, what would it be? Think very specifically about the one message you want them to grasp about money. This is really important so focus on it. Write that message down below and make sure you phrase it in a positive way.

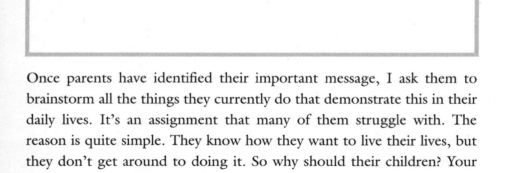

Once parents have identified their important message, I ask them to brainstorm all the things they currently do that demonstrate this in their daily lives. It's an assignment that many of them struggle with. The reason is quite simple. They know how they want to live their lives, but they don't get around to doing it. So why should their children? Your children are never too young to start. Once they get the hang of it, they come up with lots of ideas of their own. The only challenge, then, is in finding the time and commitment to do it and actually making it happen.

Here's the Money Message Wheel that one of my dads completed. The message he wanted to send to his children was, 'Time is more important than money.'

At least once this week, leave work in time to put Paul to bed.

Give time to Paul when just the two of us.

Stop buying sweets to give Paul when I get in from work.

Spend time with Paul creating a tape recording for his mum's birthday.

Find a good book to read to him with this message – ask at local bookshop.

Stop buying Paul a treat every time we go to the shops.

Stop bribing Paul by promising toys if he behaves.

Action

Focus on the money message that you want to send to your children. In the Money Message Wheel overleaf, brainstorm all the things that you can do to live that message in your own life – and to send a positive message to your child.

Once you have completed the wheel, rank your ideas from one to seven.

1. _____

2. _____

MONEY MESSAGE

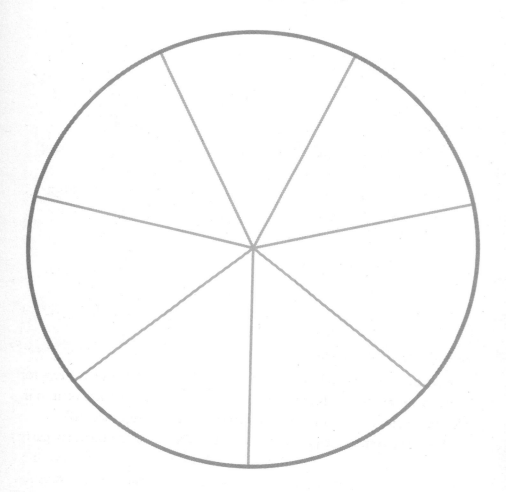

3. _____

4. _____

5. _____

6. _____

7. _____

■ What idea is top of your list?

■ What makes that idea the big one for you?

You now have seven great ways of sending your children an important message about money and value. Focus on one idea a day. Put it into your diary and make it happen.

DAY 5: DON'T LET THEIR BIRTHDAY PUT YEARS ON YOU

The thorny topic of children's birthday parties causes so much stress for so many mums and dads that I'm devoting a day of our action plan to it. Please read it, even if your child's birthday is a little distance off.

It's hard to imagine just how fearful the spectre of the birthday party can become – or perhaps not, if you've experienced it in your own life. Well, today is the day that you begin to take control and send that spectre packing.

Life is far too short. Don't let worries about their birthday parties put years on you. It just isn't worth it.

With the mums that I coach, birthday stress has two main causes. Firstly, the cost of funding it. Secondly, dealing with large numbers of children, their parents and often other siblings. And that's not to mention the mess in the house – if you're feeling brave enough to have the party at home.

One of my clients, Laura, was particularly anxious about her little one, Clara's, imminent third birthday. Clara had been to lots of parties during the year. Laura had lots of friends with children Clara's age – and then there were all of her friends at the nursery. On top of that, Clara's brother, William, who was six expected to have some of his friends along too. Well before the birthday arrived, Laura could feel herself ageing!

When I asked her how she imagined the birthday party might be, she described a vision similar to the many parties Clara had been to. There were loads of children and parents. Volume was at an all-time high. Nobody was doing what they were supposed to. She worried about looking after the other mums and dads and worried about what they thought of her apparent lack of control. The whole place was a mess. It was something Laura just wanted to be over and done with, and be glad when it was behind her.

Sound familiar? Stop right there. The first step is to decide what you want the birthday party to be like. Forget everything that has gone before. If you are going to really enjoy this party – and your children are too – you need to be in control. Don't feel guilty that what you want is different from what your children want. If you are feeling happy, in control, motivated and de-stressed, you'll all enjoy this special celebration much more. That's a gift you can give to them.

Take a look at the following questions and answer them. In an ideal world (to maximise your enjoyment and energy and keep stress levels as low as possible):

■ How many children would be there?
■ Who would those children be?
■ How many adults do you want to help you?
■ Who would they be?
■ Where would the party be?
■ How long would it last?
■ What would be the ideal schedule for that time? Write it down in detail.

- ■ Who would help you?
- ■ What specifically could you ask the other mums and dads to do that would make your life easier and not more difficult?
- ■ What is the maximum you want to spend?
- ■ What do you want to spend that budget on? Write it down in detail.

When Laura completed this exercise, she came up with a very different party from the one she'd previously described. She wanted just five other children so that she could have the party at home. She wanted the party to last for one and a half hours only. She wanted the party to be themed 'Thomas The Tank Engine' because that was Clara's favourite. The maximum she wanted to spend was £40. Laura found this very liberating. She knew just from talking about this party that she – and Clara – would really enjoy it. So what was stopping her from delivering it?

Laura was concerned what other parents would think. After all, Clara had been to their parties. How could she invite some friends and not others? What would people say about her? Would it mean the invitations for Clara dried up?

I asked Laura what she could do to deal with this challenge. Laura said that she knew the smaller party was the way to go for all the right reasons. She decided that the best way was to tackle it head on. She sent out the invitations and rehearsed what she was going to say to friends who may have been expecting one. She practised being very positive about her decision and explaining why she'd decided to do it this way. Rather than worrying about what the other parents were thinking about her – or saying behind her back – she decided that she would grasp the nettle.

Laura called me the following week to say how relieved she felt. The party was on the coming Saturday and she was looking forward to it. And the response from other parents? Well, the majority of them congratulated her on the decision and said they wished they'd done that. Many of them said how stressful they'd found throwing their children's party and were now committed to following Laura's example next time. She'd started a trend – and I know it'll become very popular. There was only one parent who took offence, and her negative response was really about her and how she feels about herself. It had nothing to do with the birthday.

Action

Focus on what you want to get out of your children's birthday parties. How do you want to feel at the end of the day to know that they have been successful. What criteria will you set?

Now take a look at the following questions and answer them.

- How many children would be there?
- Who would those children be?
- How many adults do you want to help you?
- Who would they be?
- Where would the party be?
- How long would it last?
- What would be the ideal schedule for that time? Write it down in detail.
- What, specifically could you ask the other mums and dads to do that will make your life easier and not more difficult?
- What is the maximum you want to spend?
- What do you want to spend that budget on? Write it down in detail.
- How will you tell the people you want to invite?

You now have the beginning of your action plan. These are the key decisions. Now that they have been made, you can move forwards – and enjoy a birthday celebration to remember.

DAY 6: DON'T GO CHRISTMAS CRACKERS

'I'll be glad when it's over. I'll never get everything done by Christmas. Their presents are costing a fortune and I don't know how we'll manage.' These were some of the comments I heard from a mum I coached recently – and I hear these sentiments again ... and again ... and again.

For children, Christmas is the most exciting time of the year. For parents, it is often the most challenging. Energy levels hit an all-time low. Stress levels hit an all-time high. And you just know there aren't enough hours in the day.

You've spent hours making a halo to turn Alicia into an angel for the nursery play. But she throws a tantrum – and the halo – because Colin says it looks like a doughnut. The Christmas cards are in a 'safe place' but you can't remember where. The tree isn't so much decorated as distressed and every room in the house looks like a crime scene. The ads on Cartoon Network seem longer than the programmes and every time James sees a new toy, he screams until it's added to his Christmas list. He even uses the TV jargon, 'but mum, it's only £49.99!!' You've no idea how to begin to plan Christmas lunch, especially as your teenage niece is adamant she'll only eat the 'Atkins' way. You're on a diet and the in-laws are couch potatoes. Another credit card bill arrives, but this time you don't even open it. And you're late leaving the house. It's tough trying to be the perfect parent – especially at Christmas.

TAKE CONTROL OF CHRISTMAS

Do you feel in control of Christmas – or does it just happen to you? The less in control you feel, the more stressed you will be. Put yourself back in the driving seat by taking control of Christmas spending! This is the area that most parents identify as the major cause of family pressure – and the one they are still paying for, months afterwards.

Decide how much money you want to spend this Christmas. Remember, this is a positive decision, not a negative one. Discuss it with whoever you want to. Make a detailed list of Christmas expenses – such as presents, decorations, food – and say exactly how much money you want to spend on each item on the list. Make the financial challenge fun.

The consumer madness and mayhem of Christmas can make life complicated for you. It's a time when we talk about the importance of giving but frankly the children seem much more interested in receiving. This is where you start getting creative with your presents. Make a list of all of the values that are important to you as a parent. Identify the top three.

1.

> 2.

> 3.

- What makes these so vital in your family life?
- How high does the 'money value' come on your list?
- Think about your best Christmas ever. What made it special?
- What would you really love to do with your children this Christmas?
- What do you want them to remember for years to come? Think memory, not money.
- What do you need to do to make it happen? Draw up your Christmas Memory Action List – and do it.

Action

Put an entry in your diary for sometime in November to go through this chapter and act on it. I know that's a busy time of year, but this won't take long. And I can assure you it will be time well spent – you'll certainly reap the benefits.

DAY 7: FAMILY BUDGET UPDATE

You have now reached day seven of your action plan. By completing each of the daily exercises you will have come a long way in establishing a strategy that will help you move forwards.

By now you have

- Committed to making money a liberator, not a dictator.
- Started your life bank balance and begun to appreciate the value, rather than the cost, of things.

■ Begun to take control of your family purse strings with a strategic action plan.

■ Created a plan to teach your children the message you want them to learn about the value of money.

■ Made some great decisions about your children's next birthday.

■ Committed to taking control of Christmas instead of going Christmas crackers.

This week, I asked you how stressed you felt about money. On a scale of 1 to 10, how stressed do you feel about money – or lack of it – today? A rating of 1 indicates low level of stress. A rating of 10 indicates a high level of stress. What rating did you give yourself then? What rating do you give yourself now? Circle the number below that applies.

1   2   3   4   5   6   7   8   9   10

I also asked you to rank on a scale of 1 to 10, how much you feel in control of your finances at the moment? A rating of 1 indicates a low level of control and a rating of 10 indicates a high level of control. What rating did you give yourself at the beginning of the week? What rating do you give yourself now?

1   2   3   4   5   6   7   8   9   10

If you have followed the 7-day action plan, you will have noticed significant changes in the way you feel about finance. It may still be very challenging – but you are in control and moving forwards. Think about how you felt at the beginning of the week and how you feel today.

■ What has been the biggest challenge for you this week?

■ What is the biggest positive difference in the way you feel today compared with the feelings you experienced at the beginning of the week?

■ What positive impact has the new regime had on you and everyone in your family?

■ How does that feel?

Action

Read your Parent Achievement Log (see page 291) for this week and recognise all that you have achieved as you have risen to the challenge of your family budget. Take your time and enjoy the feeling of achievement. Focus on the difference you are making to yourself and to your family by thinking and acting positively and taking control as you make money a liberator, not a dictator in your life.

Now rank your achievements from one to seven with number one being the achievement that has had the biggest impact on you and your family this week.

1. _____

2. _____

3. _____

4. _____

5. _____

6. _____

7. _____

- What makes this your biggest achievement of the week?
- What impact has it had on you?
- What impact has it had on your relationship with your children?
- How does that feel?

Your life bank balance is the most important bank balance you have. Every day, remember to keep adding to it and enjoy watching that life balance grow.

chapter eleven
energise all your relationships

'Mum! Can you watch me do this please .... now Mum!'

'Let's have an early night tonight, darling ....'

'Would it be all right if I dropped Poppy off with you for a couple of hours ...?'

'It needs to be finished before you leave work ...'

'Dad and I hardly ever see the grandchildren ...'

Sometimes it's the people who are closest to you that can put you under the greatest pressure. They are the people you love and really care for – and they all want a part of you. They may be your children, partner, friends, colleagues or relatives. They all want a piece of the action. And the action is you.

Lots of mums and dads get worried because there's only so much of them to go round – and it never seems to be quite enough. You're trying your hardest to please everyone because all these relationships matter to you. But you feel as though you're pleasing no one. There's certainly no time for you to think about yourself – in fact, you've forgotten what you're really like. It's been such a long time since you had a moment to yourself. An early night – you must be joking! Making love may be at the top of his agenda but it's at the bottom of your 'to do' list. You're far too tired for any of that by the time you get to bed. Your ideal early night is just that – children asleep and your chance to get in a few hours before your toddler makes her regular alarm call at around 2am.

As a parent, you're the driving force behind a whole range of very important relationships with yourself, your partner (if you have one), children, colleagues, relatives and friends. They can be the most rewarding relationships in your life, but if you feel negative about them and think that you're under-performing or that they're out of control, they can also be the most stressful. These relationships can be demanding even at the best of times. But once you become a parent your whole world turns upside down. You have a little person who's totally dependent on you. It can often seem that, no matter how hard you try, you just don't have enough energy or time to fit everyone else in.

The more you worry about letting people down, the worse it gets. You can even start feeling guilty when you've got nothing to feel guilty about.

All strong relationships need working at and that includes being a parent. When you become a mum or dad, you start on a very steep learning curve. Some parents say to me, 'I'm not a natural parent – I have to work at it.' In my experience, all parents who want to be the best parents possible will always be working at it. It's a roller-coaster ride. It's fun and exciting – and scary and challenging. Relationships don't just happen. The best relationships are the ones that you are constantly investing in. But, at times, the idea of investing positive time and energy in those relationships can make you feel tired just thinking about it – especially if the relationships are demanding ones.

This week, we are going to focus on your key relationships and look at ways that you can make positive changes in them that will reduce your stress and boost your energy. By getting this right, you can make a huge difference in all areas of your life.

I want you to start by thinking about the values that are most important to you in your relationships. Identify your top three values.

1.

2.

3.

What is it that makes those values particularly important to you? Your values are your driving force. If you are living them in every area of your life, you will be energised. If you are not living them, for whatever reason, you will feel stressed.

Take a look at the Relationship Table below. Give each relationship a score out of 10. A rating of 10 indicates that this relationship is exactly how you want it. A rating of one indicates that there's quite a bit of room for improvement, and major changes would have a positive impact on your life. This is a subjective judgement. If you are giving a relationship a mark of one, it doesn't meant that it is 'bad' – you're just saying it needs working at if you want to move closer to a 10. Your relationship with yourself is included in the table, so think about that first.

Relationship	Rating out of 10
Me	
My children	
My partner (or lack of one)	
My friends	
My relatives	

- Which relationship do you find most stressful?
- Which relationship takes up most of your energy?
- Which relationship is most rewarding?
- How do you score your relationship with yourself?
- In which relationship would making changes have the biggest positive impact on you?
- What difference has each of these relationships made in your life?

Now, focus on each of the relationships in turn and consider its rewards and challenges.

- What is the single most positive thing about each relationship – what do you value most?
- What is the greatest challenge?

Relationship	Positive	Challenge
Me		
My children		
My partner (or lack of one)		
My friends		
My relatives		

The important thing to remember this week is that you can only work on yourself. You can take control of what you do and how you respond, but you cannot change other people – adults or children. They need to make those changes themselves. What you can do is change the way you are. This will affect the dynamic of your relationships and can bring about significant positive changes in other people.

As we go through the week, we're going to focus on each of these key relationships in turn. Every relationship needs to be worked at if it is to grow and flourish. Even if you are really happy with how things are at the moment, take a look at these ideas and create a plan to make your good relationships even better.

Teaching your children the value of positive relationships is a gift they'll carry with them through life. It's never too young to start.

Action

Focus again on what you value most about each of those relationships – with yourself, your partner (if you have one), friends, children and relatives.

- When was the last time you told them what you value in your relationship with them?
- How do you feel when people tell you what they value in their relationship with you?

Over the course of this week, I'd like you to tell these people what you value most about your relationships with them. Choose one person in each of the categories – including yourself. Be as specific as you can.

It's really important that we acknowledge our achievements as parents. Each day I want you to make a note of your biggest achievement (see Parent Achievement Log, page 291). It may be something you achieve when you're carrying out your daily coaching action. Or it may be something that just happens in the course of the day and you think to yourself, 'Yes! That was great!' You decide what is significant for you.

DAY 2:
LOOKING AFTER YOU

Where did you come in your relationship priorities? You should be at the top. You're the driving force in so many relationships. If you are feeling energised and motivated, this will impact on all the relationships in every area of your life. It's vital that you look after yourself – and I mean **really** look after yourself. Mums, especially first-time mums, find this a very challenging concept. They're particularly great at looking after everybody else, but not so good at looking after themselves. Everybody else comes first. Mums come last.

By putting yourself low down on your list of priorities, all your relationships are affected. You are just too tired and too stressed to inject energy and enthusiasm into them. If you put yourself and your needs last, everyone will suffer – especially you. Putting yourself first isn't selfish at all. It is a must. How committed are you to doing it? It will have a significant impact on you as a person and as a parent. It will have a direct impact on your relationship with your children.

I'd like you to think for a moment about the real you. What makes you tick? Don't think in terms of you as a partner or a parent or a son or a daughter. Think about you.

- Who are you?
- What do you want?
- What feelings are important to you?

In the Real Me Wheel opposite, write one word in each section that describes what you want for the real you. Close your eyes and just think about that for a couple of minutes. It can be quite challenging, after all, the luxury of thinking about yourself is just that – a luxury. You probably don't do it very often, and may not have done it for years. Relax and enjoy the moment. Get back in touch with you. Remember, this is about you and how you feel. It's not about what other people think of you.

Kelly, a client of mine, completed her wheel with the following words: Adventurous, Energetic, Positive, Confident, Secure, Motivated, Pioneering and Creative.

'That's the real me,' she said. 'That's how I was when I was at school.' I asked her how many of those words applied to the Kelly of today. 'None,' she said. 'They've all disappeared.'

As you fill in each segment of your wheel, think carefully about what you are writing. What makes that word so important to you? Now rank

REAL ME

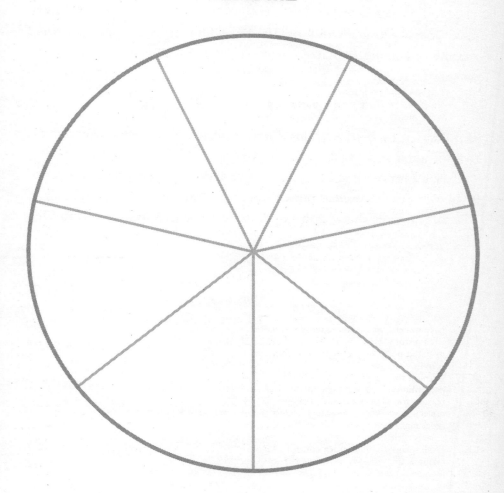

each of these words in order of their importance to you. Choose the one that is most important to you to have in your life. They will all be significant for you in some way but focus on the top one.

- How strong is that feeling in your life at the moment?
- How often do you feel it?

Give yourself a mark out of 10 depending on the following scale: a rating of 1 indicates that you never feel it and a rating of 10 means that you always feel it.

1 2 3 4 5 6 7 8 9 10

If you haven't scored a 10, just imagine what a difference it would make to your life if you could.

Make a list of three things that you can do to improve your score. So, if you want to feel excited but you only get that feeling sometimes, make a list of the three things you can do to increase that feeling in your life.

```
1.
```

```
2.
```

```
3.
```

Terri, one of my mums put 'fun' as the feeling she'd most like to have in her life. She said she'd forgotten how to have fun herself – and she was so tense with her family that the enjoyment had gone out of being a mum. She gave herself a 'fun' score of 1 – so lots of room for improvement. Now, don't get me wrong. She had beautiful twins, Amelia and

Hugo, and a wonderful husband, Tom. She loved being a mum. But when she stopped to think about the real Terri, she realised that the carefree, fun-loving Terri had been replaced by a serious, tense Terri. When had the change occurred? Terri said she knew exactly when – from the moment she became a mum. She still wanted to have fun, but life looked different now. She couldn't remember the last time that she giggled. She was a real giggler as a child. She said that her husband had once said to her, 'The best thing about you, Terri, is your sense of fun. You just light up a room.' Terri admitted that the bulb certainly needed changing!

She identified the following three things that would make her feel more like the old, fun-loving Terri.

1. Laugh. Just do it, especially with the children. She couldn't remember the last time she'd had a real laugh – even when she was enjoying herself playing with them.
2. Be a child again with the twins. She wanted to see life through their eyes and experience their sense of wonder and excitement.
3. Organise a babysitter so that she and Tom could have time together.

These were simple ideas and were extremely easy to integrate into her life. They made a big difference to Terri. She made a conscious effort to laugh out loud and to get back in touch with how it felt. She started to enjoy being childlike herself with the twins and to wonder at the world through their eyes. She organised a babysitter and went out with Tom. They let their hair down and had fun – just like the old times. They hadn't been out on their own since the twins were born.

Action

Take a look at your Real Me Wheel and, in particular, the segment that you identified as the key one you want to work on. What one thing can you do that will boost that feeling in your life today? Commit to doing it in the next 24 hours.

■ What difference will it make if you do it?

■ How will you feel?

■ What impact will it have on your relationship with yourself?

Put your Real Me Wheel somewhere easily visible. Take each word a day at a time and identify one action you can take to turbo-boost the real you. By this time next week, you'll notice a significant difference in your relationship with you. Real me – here I come.

DAY 3: YOU AND YOUR CHILDREN

Today, we're going to focus on your relationship with your children. It's likely to be one of the most special relationships you will ever have in your life, and nobody can really imagine what it is like for you. There's a very special bond between you and them. They love you unconditionally. They've changed your life forever.

Many of the mums and dads I coach just love being parents and are so committed to being the best mums and dads possible – even when the going is tough. Think about that special relationship you have with your children. Sometimes, we're so busy doing everything that we don't take the time to reflect on just what a wonderful relationship this is. What makes your relationship with your children so special?

When you're with them today, give them a cuddle and tell them just how special that relationship is to you and what makes them so special. It doesn't matter if they're not talking yet – I want you to hear yourself saying these things out loud to them.

It doesn't matter how great your relationship is with your children, every parent I've ever worked with wants to make it even better. Parents say this is the most important job they'll ever do in their lives – and they want to give it their all.

Carrie is a mum with two children, Harry, who is four, and Emily, who is nearly two. Carrie wanted to focus on her relationship with Harry and how she could improve that. Emily had been quite a sickly baby and Harry was always quite independent. Carrie had a sense that Harry was missing out because she wasn't giving him as much attention. The two children had begun to have some terrible arguments, as small children do, with Harry usually coming off worst. Carrie also knew that she was in the habit of saying, 'Come on Harry, you're older than Emily. You should know better', and even, 'Oh, just give it to her Harry, I can't have another argument.' Harry, a very wise four year-old, had even pointed this out to Carrie. 'Do you know, Mum, you spend a lot more time with Emily. We always do what she wants to do. It's not fair. I wish we could do things – just the two of us.' Sometimes it can take a small child to give us the wake-up call that gets us to act.

This is what Carrie's Relationship Wheel looked like:

Carrie looked at her wheel and said she felt good just writing those things down. She felt positive about taking the time and space to think about her relationship with Harry. She knew she wanted to do something about this with Harry, but just hadn't got around to it. They were all quite easy things for her to do and she acted on them.

Take a look at your Relationship With Your Children Wheel opposite. In each of the segments, I want you to write down one thing that you can do to make that relationship even better, even stronger than it is at the moment.

Everything you put into the wheel must be a positive thing that you can do and that is within your control. Write down what you will do – rather than what you won't do. This means that instead of writing, for example, 'stop shouting so much', put 'ignore his bad behaviour' or 'keep calm' or 'praise him for doing something well'.

Action

Now fill in your wheel. If you have more than one child, focus on one at a time.

Well done. You've just identified seven great ideas that will boost your relationship with your children in a very positive way. Take a look at them and rank them from one to seven with number one being the idea you'd most like to put into practice straight away.

1. _____

2. _____

3. _____

4. _____

5. _____

6. _____

7. _____

RELATIONSHIP WITH YOUR CHILDREN

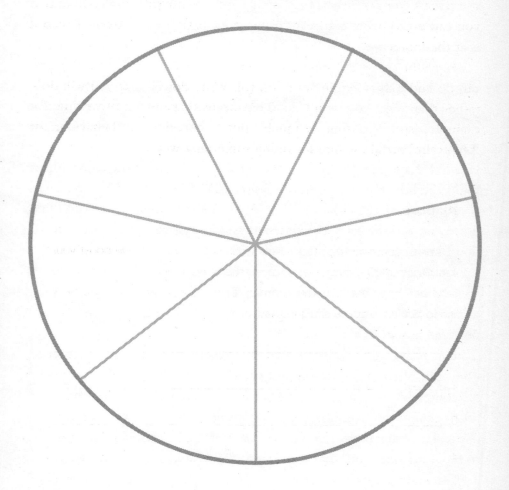

- What makes number one such a strong one for you?
- What difference will it make to you and to your children?
- What difference will it make to your relationship?

Once you have your list, put each action in your diary – a day at a time. You have seven ideas in front of you, one for each day of the week. Now all you need to do is to make sure that they happen.

DAY 4:
YOU AND YOUR PARTNER

Kate is the mother of George, who is three, and Amelia who is nearly one year old. Kate says, 'Jacob just doesn't seem to realise how much I have to do and how tired I am. He always seems to be criticising me and keeps accusing me of giving him jobs to do. I'm just trying to get everything done. He says he feels he comes way down on my list of priorities. I don't know what's happened to us.'

Jacob is Kate's partner and the father of George and Amelia. Jacob says, 'What happened to the woman I married? Kate used to be such great company and we'd talk for hours. Now she's become sleep-deprived and neurotic.'

Our relationship with our partners – whether you are still together or not – can often cause stresses and strains. Having a family changes your life completely – in a great way – but it also has an impact on many other relationships. Sometimes, the relationship with your partner can be particularly vulnerable. Everyone's relationships are different. I want you to focus on what you can do to improve this area of your life today.

You and your partner are a team. You both share the responsibility of bringing up your children. Whatever your family situation – whether you are together, or separated, or divorced – this relationship needs working at. If you are to move forwards it needs to be a win-win relationship.

Begin today by focusing on your partner and answering the following questions:

- What are your partner's most positive qualities?
- What makes him/her a good dad/mother?
- What is your partner's most significant achievement as a parent?

Now share these thoughts with your partner. You can choose how you do it. Phone, or send a text, a note or a card. Or say it to your partner face to face. The decision is yours.

Every day this week, I want you to look at your partner and see the things you love about him or her – even when it's most challenging. Don't see the negatives. See the positives, even if you have to look quite hard.

It's good to get into the habit of doing this, not only with your partner but with your children as well – especially when they're at their most challenging.

This is a good exercise, too, if you are working at improving your relationship with your partner following a separation or divorce. Having a negative relationship will not help you or your children – so do what you can to boost the positives and you will all reap the benefits.

This is what Kate's Relationship with Partner Wheel looked like:

Kate decided that spending time together was top of her list and she did arrange to go to a football match with Jacob. To say he was shocked was an understatement, but they really enjoyed their time together.

Some couples I coach have never been out since they had children and this puts a huge amount of pressure on them. Give yourselves some time and space in a child-free zone. Even if it's just for an hour, arrange for someone to look after the children and enjoy each other's company. My challenge to you – talk about anything you like, but not the children!

Action

Complete your own Relationship with Partner Wheel opposite, write down seven actions that you can take to improve your relationship with your partner. Now take a look at that list and rank each of your ideas from one to seven with number one being the idea you'd most like to put into effect today.

You have your strategy, so make it happen. Action one thing from your list every day this week. By making small changes every day, you'll find you can make a big positive difference to your relationship in just one week.

As you're implementing your plan, notice how your partner responds when you are taking positive actions that involve them.

■ How does that feel?
■ What impact is it having on your relationship?

DAY 5: RELATIVES AND FRIENDS – OR FIENDS?

Your relationships with your relatives and friends can be the most rewarding – and the most challenging. I work with many clients who find that relatives and closest friends can create the worst problems and drain their energy most. When communication breaks down, stress sets in.

RELATIONSHIP WITH PARTNER

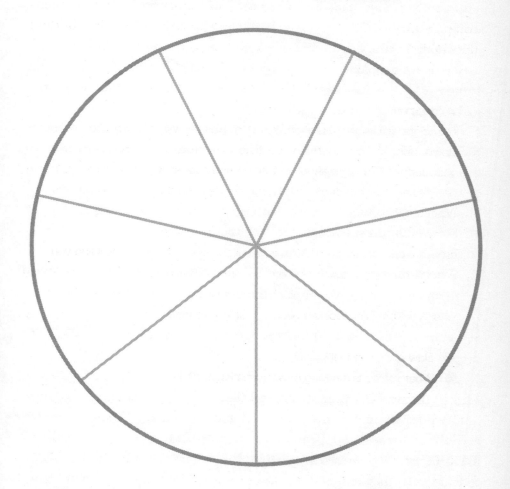

The next step for you is to focus on this area of your life and be very clear with yourself about how you want to invest your time and energy. It's often the case that as we go along in life, we can find ourselves surrounded by relatives or friends we've known for years and who we feel close to, in many ways, but who are actually having a negative impact on our lives, and this causes stress. If you want to change this situation you can. You are in control of your life. Don't let them control you.

Today, I want you to take stock and focus on surrounding yourself with positive people whom have a positive effect on your life. I want you to take a long hard look at the people you spend your time with and make some tough – but great decisions.

In the Relatives and Friends Wheel opposite, write down the names of the seven people whom you most enjoy spending time with. Make sure that you include the people who have a really positive impact on you.

■ What's special about your relationship with each of these people?
■ How often do you see or speak to them?
■ How often would you like to?
■ Who is the one person on that list that, if you saw them or spoke to them more often, would have the biggest positive impact on you?

Sometimes, however, we think we're spending time with 'friends' – and they're actually 'fiends'!

Now complete your Relatives and Fiends Wheel on page 278. Make a list of the people whom you spend time with or invest energy in who have a negative impact on you and drain your energy. Think carefully here about 'friends' you spend time with only because they have children the same age as yours. When many of my clients do this exercise they conclude that they're spending lots of time with people just because they have children the same age. Be rigorous in your friendship audit in deciding what works for you.

■ What negative effect do they have on you?
■ How often do you see or speak to these people?

RELATIVES AND FRIENDS

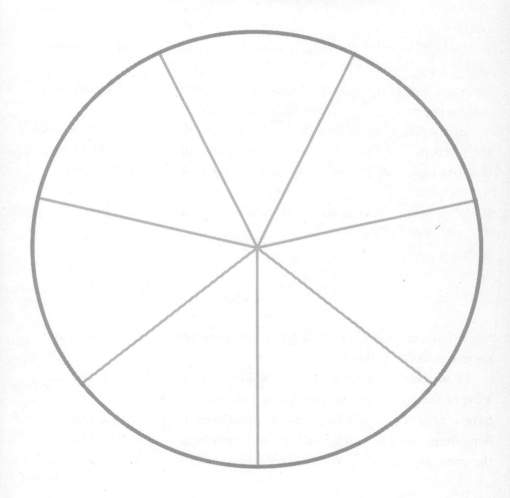

RELATIVES AND FIENDS

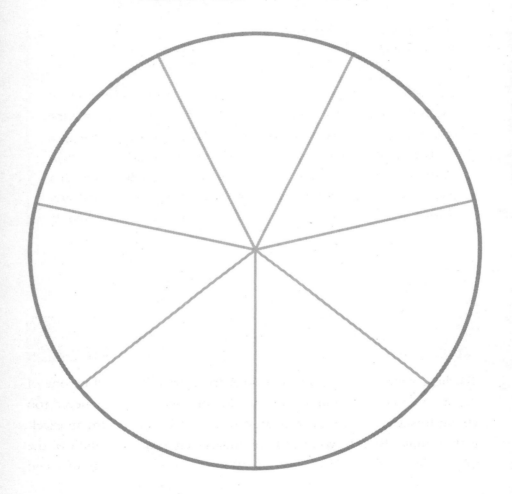

■ How often would you like to?

■ Who is the one person who has the biggest negative effect on you?

Action

Today, commit to filling your life with positive people and feel yourself grow.

■ Who was the number one on your priority list?

■ How often would you like to see or speak to them?

Call them now and have a chat or put a date in your diary. Plan ahead. If your best friend lives in a different part of the country – arrange some dates now to get together later in the year. Take control and boost your energy.

Don't waste time on people you feel you ought to be with or who you're afraid to say 'no' to. Life is too short. Time is at a premium for you as a parent so make wise choices. If you think the friendship is worth investing in – invest. If not, move on. Make room in your life for other people who do deserve your time and energy.

DAY 6: TEACH YOUR CHILDREN THE VALUE OF FRIENDSHIP

Teaching your children positive lessons about friendship will be one of the most important things you can do for them. They're never too young to start. You are their greatest role model, so set them an excellent example. By now you will have undertaken a rigorous audit of the people close to you and will have developed a positive strategy to spend more time with people who boost your energy and reduce your stress levels – and less time with those who drain your energy and boost your stress levels.

Focus on the values that are important in your friendships and the qualities that they bring out in you. Think about the messages you want to send your children about their growth as a friend and their friendships.

Begin by focusing on your children's great qualities as a friend and make a list of them.

- What do you love most about their character?
- What aspects would you like to develop and build on?

One of my clients, Cal, was nervous about Katie, her young daughter, who was starting school. Cal said she was more nervous than Katie and she wanted to be prepared. She wanted to build Katie's confidence so that her daughter would enjoy the experience and make new friends. Cal also needed to prepare herself. She'd been at home with Katie longer than she had with her other children.

Here is Cal's Friendship Wheel for Katie:

I asked Cal to prioritise the qualities from one to seven. She ranked 'kindness' at the top. I asked Cal to think of practical ways to boost Katie's 'kindness' quality. Cal said it made her focus on how important her example is. She decided to make a real effort to praise Katie when she was kind. When Katie was unkind, Cal would be specific about what was unhelpful about this behaviour. This was a change from the norm. Usually Cal would just tell her off if she was being unkind.

Cal was happy with this plan. It meant Katie would learn something very positive about friendship. Cal also looked at practical ways of building Katie's confidence so that she'd be well placed to make friends. Cal also committed to stop saying, 'I'll miss you when you start at the school.' She realised she was saying this a lot – and didn't want Katie to end up worrying about her mum! Cal decided to stop saying anything negative and concentrate on being positive about the fun new things they were both going to do.

Complete your own Child Friendship Wheel overleaf. I want you to identify the key friendship qualities that you want to strengthen in your children. Be as specific as possible.

Action

Now look at your Child Friendship Wheel overleaf. Think carefully about the qualities that you want to strengthen in your little one.

Once you have completed the wheel, rank the qualities from one to seven with number one being the quality you identify as being the most important to develop.

1. _____

2. _____

3. _____

4. _____

CHILD FRIENDSHIP

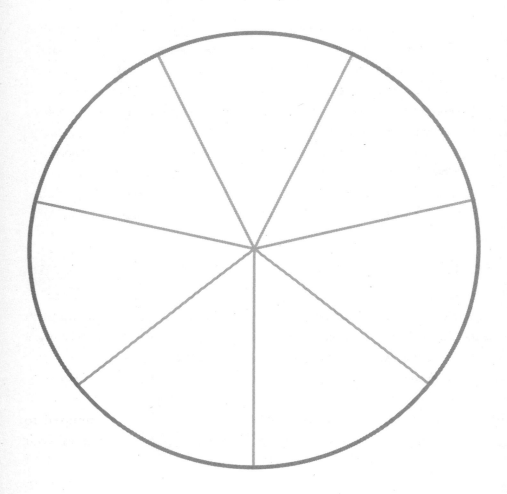

5. _____

6. _____

7. _____

What practical step can you take to help boost that quality in your children? Be as specific and creative as you can. You now have seven qualities to enhance. Put one a day into your diary and focus on practical ways of boosting these in your children. It will be a great exercise for you and them and by this time next week, you'll feel you've made significant steps forwards.

Don't leave something as important as being a good friend to chance. Take control and give your children a gift they'll treasure throughout life.

DAY 7: RELATIONSHIP UPDATE

You have now reached day seven of your action plan. By completing each of the daily exercises you will have come a long way in establishing a strategy that will help you to energise your relationships.

By now you have:

■ Started to get back in touch with the real you and committed to putting that key relationship with yourself at the top of your priorities.

■ Acknowledged the values that are important to you in relationships and recognised relationships that have a positive and negative effect on you.

■ Developed a practical plan to make your relationship with your children even more special.

■ Identified ways of boosting your relationship with your partner by focusing on their positives.

■ Made important decisions about your relatives and friends to ensure you spend your time with positive people.

■ Taken practical action to teach your children about the value of friendship.

At the beginning of the week I asked you to give each of your significant relationships a rating out of 10. In how many of these relationships have you made positive changes over the past week?

Relationship	I have made positive changes
Me	
My children	
My partner (or lack of one)	
My friends	
My relatives	

If you have followed the 7-day action plan, you will have noticed significant changes in all your major relationships – especially your relationship with yourself. Think about how you felt at the beginning of the week and how you feel today.

■ What has been the biggest challenge for you this week?

■ What is the biggest positive difference in the way you feel today compared with the feelings you experienced at the beginning of the week?

■ What positive impact has the new regime had on you and everyone in your family?

Action

Read your Parent Achievement Log (see page 291) for this week and recognise all that you have achieved. Take your time and enjoy the feeling of achievement. Focus on the difference you are making to yourself and to your family by thinking and acting positively and taking control of the important relationships in your life. As we said at the beginning of the week, your relationship with yourself is the key to every other relationship in your life. Look after yourself and nurture your relationship with yourself and ensure your positive development as a parent. Now rank your achievements from one to seven with number one being the achievement that has had the biggest impact on you and your family this week.

1. _____

2. _____

3. _____

4. _____

5. _____

6. _____

7. _____

- What makes this your biggest achievement of the week?
- What impact has it had on you?
- What impact has it had on your relationship with your child?
- How does that feel?

Remember that you need to work on all your relationships if they are to grow and flourish. You are on a journey, so enjoy it. You can take all the skills and techniques that you have put into practice this week and apply them to any area of your life and to any relationship that is important to you. Keep moving forwards – especially in that all-important relationship – with yourself.

chapter twelve

make family life a daring adventure

Thank you for joining me on a journey through this book. We all know that being a parent is something like being on a white-knuckle roller-coaster ride. At times it's exciting and exhilarating and at others challenging and terrifying. Most of all, I hope that you feel you've really developed as a parent and enjoyed nurturing your relationship with yourself and your children.

As you've moved forward through the pages of this book – a day at a time – you have been taking control of your life and taking action to bring about positive changes. You've reduced your stress and increased your energy levels. You've achieved this because you are passionate about being a great parent. You recognise that it's the most rewarding, challenging and important job you'll ever do in your life. You're motivated and committed to being the best mum or dad that you can be. You're not just talking about it – you're doing it.

As you've created your very own action plan, you've come to recognise what you know already, that you are the expert on your own family situation and you know what you want to achieve and the best way to achieve it. You know what you want for yourself and your family. You've identified effective, easy-to-implement ideas to tackle your top practical and emotional problems. You've started to live your life in a different way. You have nurtured your positive inner parent – you believe in yourself and your ability to be the best parent possible. You laugh, you're optimistic, energetic, dynamic, creative and passionate. You've created a world that is full of inventive solutions, not problems. You've given yourself the time and the space to focus on your family values and goals – and you've achieved a huge amount on a daily basis. Just think back to how you were feeling when your started your journey.

- What was that like?
- How far do you think you have come?
- What's been your greatest achievement over the past few weeks?
- How does that feel?

Not only have you been coaching yourself, you have implemented a great strategy to coach your children. You're building their confidence, giving them self-belief and establishing positive values, skills and qualities in them that they will carry through adult life. These are the greatest gifts a parent can give their children.

You know now that in order to arrive at your chosen destination in life, you need to know where you want to be and create a step-by-step route map to get there. You've come such a long way and you still have a great deal to look forward to. Remember, there is no such thing as a perfect child or a perfect parent. Every day you are achieving a huge amount. Commit to being a positive parent and to doing the very best you can for the children that you love and you will all move forwards. What's most important is that you are in the driving seat, so prepare now to make the rest of your family life an exciting and daring adventure.

I want you to take a little time now to think about your future and what the years ahead hold for you and your family.

Just stop to think for a few minutes about yourself in the future. Imagine that you are now well into your 70s, in the evening of your life. Your children are grown up and have families of their own. Picture yourself in as much detail as you can.

- You're surrounded by your wonderful family. How does that feel?
- What would you like your son or daughter to say is the best thing about having you as a mum or a dad?

■ What do they love most about you?

■ How would you like them to describe you to their own children?

■ How would that make you feel?

■ What steps can you take to make sure that happens?

■ If you could ask your future self just one question, what would it be?

■ What would be your answer?

Imagine that you're looking back over the many years at your full and exhilarating life as a parent. Imagine that you are writing your own script about what has happened in your family life. This is your story, you are writing it – so whatever you want to happen can happen.

■ How would you describe it?

■ What have been the highlights?

■ What specific goals have you achieved over the years?

■ What experience stands out above all others as the one you will remember forever?

■ What steps can you take to make sure that happens?

Think about your children, grown up and with children of their own.

■ What kind of parent do you want them to be?

■ What values do you want them to demonstrate?

■ When they look back on their childhood, what do you want them to remember?

■ What memories have you built in them that will last forever?

■ What wonderful stories about their childhood will they share with their own children?

■ What steps can you take to make sure that happens?

Today is the first day of the rest of your life. You are in control of your life and moving forwards. Don't look back with any regrets – look forward to a wonderful future. The time you have with your children is precious, so create your own practical action plan to make life a daring adventure – and enjoy every day.

appendix
PARENT ACHIEVEMENT LOG

It's really important that we acknowledge our achievements as parents. We often do this naturally to support our children, but we don't do it for ourselves. As parents, you achieve a huge amount on a daily basis – so recognise this and celebrate it.

Each day I want you to make a note of your biggest achievement. It may be something you achieve when you're carrying out your daily coaching action. Or it may be something that just happens in the course of the day and you think to yourself, 'Yes! That was great!' You decide what is significant for you.

At the end of each week, look at your Parent Achievement Log and rank your achievements in order from one to seven, with number one being the achievement that carries the most significance for you.

Day	Biggest Achievement	Rank
1		
2		
3		
4		
5		
6		
7		

about the author

Lorraine Thomas is the UK's leading Parent Coach as featured in *The Sunday Times*, the *Daily Mail*, *You* magazine, *The Times*, the *Guardian*, the *Independent*, *Junior*, *BBC Parenting*, *Real*, *FQ* and on ITV's *This Morning*. She writes a regular monthly column for the top national magazine, *Practical Parenting*.

She is a working mother who is well aware of the challenges facing all parents and she knows from her own personal experience how coaching can transform people's lives. She gave up a career as a successful television executive to train as a coach and establish the UK's first Parent Coaching Academy.

Lorraine coaches clients in Europe, China and USA. She is much in demand as a speaker and presents seminars for parents and parenting professionals in the corporate, public and voluntary sectors. Lorraine is committed to supporting the national charity Parentalk and works with it on a range of initiatives.

Lorraine graduated from Cambridge University with a first class honours degree and is a qualified teacher. She is accredited with Distinction by The Coaching Academy in Hampshire.

Lorraine's family are her passion. She has Joshua aged 6, Holly aged 3 and an 18-year-old stepson Ben. She is married to Jerry, a broadcaster and writer.

If you would like to contact Lorraine, you can email her at:
lthomas@theparentcoachingacademy.com

index